Motivation & Learning

A Teacher's Guide to

Building Excitement for Learning

& Igniting the Drive for Quality

SPENCE ROGERS

JIM LUDINGTON

SHARI GRAHAM

PEAK LEARNING SYSTEMS, INC.

EVERGREEN, COLORADO

MOTIVATION & LEARNING

A Teacher's Guide to Building Excitement for Learning & Igniting the Drive for Quality

By

SPENCE ROGERS

JIM LUDINGTON

SHARI GRAHAM

Published by
Peak Learning Systems, Inc.
6784 S. Olympus Drive
Evergreen, CO 80439-5312
phone: (303) 679-9780
e-mail: peaklearn@aol.com
website: http://www.peaklearn.com

First Printing 1997
Second Printing 1998
Third Printing 1999

Peak Learning Systems' books may be purchased for educational or business use. For information, please call or write: Order Department, Peak Learning Systems, Inc., 6784 S. Olympus Drive, Evergreen, CO 80439-5312. Telephone: (303) 679-9780; Fax (303) 679-9781.

Portions of this book are based on an earlier resource titled *Quick Tips & Strategies to Increase Student Motivation & Learning* from Peak Learning Systems.

Clip art courtesy of Phil Frank Megatoons and CorelDraw 7.0
Cover Design by Dani Burke

Publisher's Cataloging in Publication
(Prepared by Quality Books Inc.)

Rogers, Spence.
  Motivation & learning : a teacher's guide to building excitement for learning & igniting the drive for quality / Spence Rogers, Jim Ludington, Shari Graham.
    p. cm.
  Includes bibliographical references and index.
  Preassigned LCCN: 96-72327
  ISBN: 1-889852-30-9

  1. Motivation in education. 2. Classroom management. I. Ludington, Jim. II. Graham, Shari. III. Title. IV. Title: Motivation and learning.

LB1065.R64 1997   370.1'54
                                             QBI97-40040

CONTENTS

ALPHABETICAL LISTING OF STRATEGIES AND TIPS

ABOUT THE AUTHORS

SPENCE ROGERS

Spence began his career in education over 25 years ago. Most of his efforts during this time were focused on teaching high school math, but he also served as a math department chairperson, a math curriculum coordinator, a staff-development resource teacher, a college math instructor, and more recently as a consultant to schools, districts, boards, and states.

In his role as a teacher, Spence received numerous awards that include recognition by two Arizona governors and certification on four occasions as a finalist for the Presidential Award for Excellence in Teaching Mathematics.

Spence now is the director of Peak Learning Systems and works with schools and districts in Japan, Canada, Puerto Rico, and across the United States. He is best known for his work in the area of building high performance classrooms through improving and aligning curriculum, instruction, and assessment practices at both the classroom and district levels. In addition, he provides effective staff-development in the area of enhancing student motivation. Spence is consistently recognized for his abilities to make what he teaches practical while helping others build on their strengths.

With his colleagues, Spence is the co-author of two books that are highly praised by both classroom teachers and experts in the field for their practicality and adherence to research and best known practices. His book *Motivation & Learning* is an easy to use resource designed to help teachers at all levels build challenging and motivating learning environments. It combines an easy to understand model with over 600 practical quick tips and strategies for immediate classroom use. His second book, *The High Performance Toolbox,* is a practical guidebook for successfully designing and implementing rigorous and standards-based performance tasks, projects, assessments and evaluations.

In addition to conducting staff-development workshops, Spence presents keynote addresses and both general and breakout application sessions at over a dozen major educational conferences each year. He also is a featured consultant with the National School Conference Institutes' Satellite Staff-Development Telecasts in the area of Increasing Motivation, Learning, and Performance Quality.

On a more personal side, Spence is a grandfather and lives in the Rocky Mountains near Evergreen, Colorado at over 8200 feet. He enjoys skiing and hiking with his family.

JIM LUDINGTON

Jim Ludington is an award winning math teacher and staff-developer in the Gananda Central School District in Walworth, New York. On two occasions, Jim was honored by the University of Rochester with their *Excellence in Teaching* award. He has also been named Employee of the Year by his district. In addition to fulfilling his teaching role, Jim also was a key player in the development of

Gananda's Graduation Project which has been praised by educators from around the United States and Canada.

In addition to being a practicing classroom teacher, Jim serves as a senior consultant with Peak Learning Systems. With over twenty five years of classroom experience, he brings a sense of day-to-day reality to his writing and his workshops.

Jim is a major contributor to *The Performance Learning and Assessment Toolbox*, 1st edition, and a co-author of *Quick Tips & Strategies to Improve Student Motivation and Learning* which is the predecessor to this book.

SHARI GRAHAM

Shari Graham is the 1993 Teacher of the Year for East Grand Rapids, Michigan where she served as a language arts teacher for twenty two years. She served as Assistant Director and as a senior consultant with Peak Learning Systems for two years. During this time, Shari conducted highly acclaimed staff-development workshops across the United States and Canada in the areas of performance assessment and effective instruction. She is currently the Professional Development/Assessment Consultant with the Muskegon Area Intermediate School District in Muskegon, Michigan and a senior consultant with Peak Learning Systems.

Shari is also the co-author of *The High Performance Toolbox: Succeeding with Performance Tasks, Projects, and Assessments* and *The Performance Learning and Assessment Toolbox* that preceded it. She also co-authored *Quick Tips & Strategies to Improve Student Motivation and Learning* which is the predecessor to this book.

SUE TOMASZEWSKI: CONTRIBUTING MEMBER OF THE PEAK LEARNING SYSTEMS TEAM

Though Sue has not actually served as a co-author of this book, she has been so important to our staff-development efforts and thinking that it is appropriate to recognize her here. She is a contributing author of *The Performance Learning and Assessment Toolbox*, 1st edition. She is also a staff-development specialist with the Professional Development Center of the Orleans/Niagara BOCES in Lockport, New York. In this capacity she has become a recognized expert in the areas of effective instruction, assessment, cooperative learning, motivation, classroom discipline concerns, shared decision making, and group facilitation as well as Choice Theory and Reality Therapy.

Sue has worked with inner city, suburban, and rural school districts in multi-age, self-contained, and resource room settings. She has specialized in working with the "more difficult" students and began her staff-development work as a training specialist for the New York State Special Education Training and Resource Center Network.

Currently, in addition to serving as a senior consultant with Peak Learning Systems, Sue is recognized as a faculty member of The William Glasser Institute as a Basic and Advanced Practicum Supervisor in Choice Theory and Reality Therapy.

ACKNOWLEDGMENTS

Good teaching strategies have been passed from teacher to teacher since the beginning of time. Consequently, it is impossible to determine the actual creators of many of the strategies and tips presented throughout this book. However, there are many people we would like to thank for their direct or indirect contributions.

First and foremost we would like to express our appreciation to our families for their patience and unwavering support. The strength of their convictions and their contributions to the production of *Motivation & Learning* have helped to make it a reality.

George Sisemore, in his first principalship and all his roles since, has been a continuing believer and supporter without whom this book would never have happened.

The President of The National School Conference Institute and former Superintendent of the Glendale Union High School District, Jerry George, has been instrumental in our professional development. His continued support and encouragement have been invaluable.

We would also like to thank Bill Spady for his enormous contributions to education, the opportunities he has provided us, and his support in our professional development.

Roz Rogers has tirelessly dedicated her time and energy to the publishing of this book. We are deeply indebted to her for going far beyond the call of duty.

Our special thanks and appreciation go to Lisa Pajot-Renard for her countless editing hours, writing expertise, and contributions to this edition.

Raymond Wlodkowski, Margery Ginsberg, Chuck Schwahn, and Doug Krug have been supportive role models, and contributors to our work. Their philosophies, beliefs, values, and contributions to education and leadership have been invaluable in our efforts.

Sue Tomaszewski has been an outstanding contributor to our efforts and our thinking. Thank you Sue for all you have done.

We would also like to thank the following people for their contributions, direct or indirect, to the contents of this book: Judy Aaronson, Kris Baca, Suzi Barnett, Barbara Benson, Ken Blanchard, Jim Block, Benjamin Bloom, Bob and Kathy Bocchino, John Booth, Ron Brandt, David Briggs, Dani Burke, Jim Burton,

Helen Burz, Robert Lynn Canady, Veronica Carlson, John Champlin, Susan Close, Karin Cordell, Art Costa, Stephen Covey, Bonnie Dana, Bobb Darnell, Ken Dehn, Debra DeWeerd, Jerry and Heavia Doyle, Howard Gardner, Kathy Gardner, Robert Garmston, Dan Graham, William Glasser, Rick and Shelly Grothaus, Tom Guskey, Merrill Harmin, Stephanie Harris, Mary Kay Hoffman, David Hyerle, Eric Jenson, Roger and David Johnson, Spencer Kagan, Amy Karbula, Emma Klimek, Eileen Koliba, Henry Levin, Jeanne Lokar, Suzi Loya, Kit Marshall, Robert Marzano, Margaret McCabe, Iris McGinnis, Doug McPhee, Sue Myers, Lori Nau, Christine Neal, Bea Parker, Richard Paul, Larry Pedersen, Mark Pellegrino, Jim Pfieffer, Robert Pike, Diane Price-Stone, James Raffini, Sandi Redenbach, Michael Rettig, Lyn Reville, Jacqueline Rhoades, Dawn Shannon, David Sousa, Rick Stiggins, Tony Stockwell, Tom Stone, Richard Strong, Becky Swanson, Roger Taylor, Michael Tillmann, Carm Tredwell, Tim Waters, Bruce Wellman, Pam Wesley, Sue Wells-Welsh, Debra White, Grant Wiggins, Pat Wolfe, Harry Wong, and all the others who have contributed so much to our professional growth.

INTRODUCTION

```
┌─────────────────────────────────┐
│        Introduction to          │
│    MOTIVATION & LEARNING        │
└─────────────────────────────────┘
     /            |            \
  Purpose                    Overview
 of the Book              of the Chapters

            How to Use
        MOTIVATION & LEARNING
```

THE PURPOSE OF *MOTIVATION AND LEARNING*

In our push for all students to be successful, we often have many questions about and desires for much needed solutions for our admirable but difficult goal.

- How often have we wished for an effective strategy to use in a particular teaching situation?

- How many times have we needed another approach after our best effort didn't hit the mark?

- How many of us have wished for ways to improve the quality of student work?

- How often have we wished for effective transitions and activities to use in block schedules and other extended teaching periods?

- And how many of us have longed for higher levels of motivation from some of our students?

This book is designed to help with all these legitimate needs. It contains principles, standards, techniques, strategies, and quick tips for achieving enhanced motivation, increased student learning, and quality in student work.

OVERVIEW OF THE CHAPTERS

Chapter One is the most important chapter in the entire book. It provides principles and standards that are essential for establishing and maintaining a highly motivating classroom. It also contains crucial information regarding the advantages and disadvantages of intrinsic and extrinsic motivators along with numerous tips for how to avoid classic demotivators. Research has shown that using isolated strategies to improve motivation in a classroom is ineffective. To be effective, the strategies and techniques need to be a part of a philosophical commitment and an on-going and consistent effort. Use Chapter One and the recommended resources by Dr. Raymond Wlodkowski, Dr. Margery Ginsberg, and Dr. William Glasser to ensure the strategies, techniques, and tips you use are consistent with best known practices and research.

Chapters Two through Seven are collections of strategies, techniques, and quick tips to improve student motivation, the quality of student work, and the level of student learning in your classroom. For these powerful and practical ideas to be effective, they need to be used in a manner consistent with the principles and standards presented in Chapter One.

Chapter Two provides a wealth of ways to:

1. establish and maintain a motivating classroom environment;

2. involve students in constructing standards of performance; and

3. develop quality practices.

Specifically, Chapter Two contains a variety of ways to develop and effectively use rubrics, provide effective feedback, use praise effectively, build a sense of community, check for causes of poor student motivation, promote self-directed behaviors, promote and support creativity, resolve conflicts, promote increased motivation to learn successfully, and promote quality and commitment in the classroom.

Chapter Three focuses on making classroom management easier while increasing motivation and performance quality. You can use the ideas included in this chapter to:

1. manage and save time and energy;

2. use visuals effectively to enhance learning;

3. plan your classroom layout and lessons in brain compatible ways;

4. use recorded music to improve learning;

5. manage questions to promote learning; and

6. increase student retention of knowledge.

Chapter Four addresses how to build higher levels of knowledge and understanding with your students. This chapter contains practical, immediately usable strategies and quick tips that are all designed to improve the students' learning and retention of knowledge, concepts, and skills. In order to facilitate the selection of these instructional strategies, they are labeled as to:

1. their best teaching uses, including anticipatory set, closure, review, and instruction of new material;

2. the type of content for which they are best suited, whether that be information, skills, conceptual understanding, or reasoning skills;

3. grade levels (elementary, middle school, or high school) at which the strategy can be effectively used;

4. whether they are particularly beneficial for use in improving learning with block schedules;

5. their ability to address multiple intelligences to increase student success; and

6. their applicability in cooperative learning classrooms.

Chapter Five focuses on how to increase the effectiveness of cooperative group work in the classroom. Included in this chapter are numerous ideas for how to:

1. assign group roles;

2. make grouping assignments;

3. manage group time;

4. promote quality work with cooperative groups;

5. improve the quality of communication within groups; and

6. wrap-up group projects.

Chapter Six includes a plethora of questions and prompts to encourage and facilitate high quality self and peer assessment of student behavior, thought processes, procedures, reasoning, and improvement efforts.

Chapter Seven provides hundreds of ideas for performance tasks that are rich and motivating. Included are both quick and complex ideas sorted by discipline and interdisciplinary focus.

HOW TO USE THIS BOOK

First, develop a thorough understanding of the principles and standards in Chapter One for enhancing student motivation to learn and succeed.

Caution: When instructional strategies are intoduced without ensuring that the theoretical foundation on which they are based is in place, most likely they will not have the desired or expected effects.

Scan Chapters Two through Seven for Strategies and Quick Tips to begin using immediately to improve student motivation, the quality of student work, and the levels of student learning. Be certain to use them in a context based on principles and standards for a motivational environment.

Use Chapters Two through Seven as you would your favorite cookbook. Turn to the index to find effective new strategies or old favorite, but forgotten, strategies and tips to use whenever you need them. The index lists each strategy according to its best uses and instructional targets.

CHAPTER 1

STUDENT MOTIVATION

BELIEFS, PRINCIPLES, & STANDARDS FOR ENHANCING STUDENT MOTIVATION

"FROM THE MOMENT WE'RE BORN, WE'RE MOTIVATED TO LEARN."

Whenever we feel a desire or need for something, we are in a state of motivation. Motivation is an internal feeling – it's the drive that someone has to do something. It is what makes teaching some students a joy and working with others so difficult.

Anyone who has taught knows the importance of student motivation. The best technology, curriculum, and assessments don't make a difference if the students don't want to learn. Great technology and curriculum may help by connecting with student interests, but if the students are more motivated to put their energy into something outside of learning, they will.

This book is based on the belief that motivation is intrinsic. From the moment we're born, we're motivated to learn. Almost without exception, every student is motivated to learn something. Unfortunately, many students are more motivated to learn things other than what we're trying to teach them. As teachers, we have seen students struggle to learn how to improve in their favorite sport, how to play a new video game, how to drive, or how to solve a problem they're having at home or on the streets. The problem is not that many students aren't motivated to learn, it's that they're not motivated to learn what we're teaching or in the way that they're being expected to learn.

If we're asking the question, "What can we do to motivate our students?" we're asking the wrong question. No one can motivate someone else, and yet, for years we've tried to motivate students. We've tried just about every trick that can be imagined. We've tried awards, points, rewards, demerits, grades, names on boards, honors, scholarships, certificates, time after school, report cards, notes to parents, calls home, stars, ribbons, money, and prizes.

Over the years, we've discovered that these extrinsic motivators can be powerful and work for short periods of time. Unfortunately, they soon become either not enough, or demotivators for many students, or both.

In the movie *Brave Heart*, we can see the power of intrinsic motivation. No matter what the potential reward or punishment, the Scotsmen could not be pulled from their quest for freedom. In the movie *Stand and Deliver*, a true story about low socio-economic students in California, we learned the power of student motivation. In this story, we saw what happened as a result of the efforts of Jaime Escalante to increase the desire of his students to learn. He convinced them of two things – that they could learn and that what he had to teach was important.

The struggle is not in how to motivate students to learn. The struggle is in creating lessons and classroom environments that focus and attract students' intrinsic motivation; thus, increasing the likelihood students will actively engage in the learning.

2

Fortunately, a lot has been learned about how to create lessons, units, and classroom situations that are "motivating." They can be designed to adhere to pre-determined standards. These standards for lessons, units, and classrooms increase the likelihood students will value the learning enough that they will choose to focus their energies on learning what is being taught.

In this book, we present powerful generalizations in the form of principles and standards for improving motivation, the quality of student work, and the level of student learning. Unfortunately, generalizations are just that – generalizations. When working with people, nothing works all the time, and nothing works with every-one. In fact, what works well one day with one student, may not work the next. However, these principles and standards do work most of the time with most students. They provide the theoretical framework to evaluate our efforts to increase motivation in our classrooms and to develop new approaches. They also help us avoid many classic errors that can be powerful demotivators for students.

THE TWO PRINCIPLES FOR MAXIMIZING STUDENT MOTIVATION FOR LEARNING IN A CLASSROOM

Principles are important rules to guide our behaviors. Therefore, principles for increasing motivation in a classroom are the underlying rules we use to plan, teach, and make classroom decisions in our attempts to increase student motivation for learning.

These principles provide direction so that students are most likely to have the feelings which tend to be present when people are in states of intrinsic motivation. The goal is that the students will legitimately feel:

- smart or capable;

- valued, important, and a part of the group;

- safe and secure;

- happy; and

- in "self-control" or autonomous.

PRINCIPLE ONE: OPERATE FROM UNDERSTANDING

Stephen Covey, the author of *Seven Habits of Highly Effective People* and *Principle-Centered Leadership,* has expressed this same thought: "Seek first to understand, then to be understood." Regardless of how it is said, the message is clear. If we are to be successful in increasing the levels of student motivation in our classroom, we must make decisions based on a total understanding of our students' needs.

PRINCIPLE TWO: MANAGE CONTEXT – NOT STUDENTS

People tend to resent being told what to do, when to do it, and how to do it. According to Dr. William Glasser, people have a basic need to feel free or independent. This need is greater for some than others, and it is greater for each of us at certain times than it is at others – but it is a need that exists. And yet, there are also times when we as students want direction from others. The challenge we face as teachers is determining when and how we can provide enough meaningful options and, at the same time, the appropriate amount of direction and control.

As one is designing lessons or units, or as one is making decisions while teaching and managing the classroom, constantly focus on establishing and maintaining conditions rather than on controlling or dominating others. Focus not on how to make students do or want to do something; instead, focus on creating situations in which students will want to do what needs to be done.

The musical lyric " . . . a spoonful of sugar makes the medicine go down" is very helpful in clarifying the principle "manage context, not students." It is not suggesting that sugar be offered as a bribe; the implied suggestion is to change the situation (context) so the child is more likely to choose to do what is desired. Note that the lyric does not suggest "watering down" the medicine, bribing the child, promising future benefits, or threatening punishment – it merely suggests changing the context. If the lyric had been written about school and not medicine, it might have been something like, "a motivating teacher helps the students to learn." The lyric would not have been "a bunch of points helps the students learn," nor "hopes of future benefits help the students learn," nor "fear of punishment helps students learn." The original lyric and the first school example presented above reflect managing context – not children. The humorous twists to the lyric represent managing students – not context.

SIX STANDARDS FOR MAXIMIZING STUDENT MOTIVATION FOR LEARNING IN A CLASSROOM

The students must believe the learning is:

Valuable	Safe
Involving	Caring
Successful	Enabling

STANDARD 1: VALUABLE

This is the most important standard. People apply themselves to the extent they believe what they are doing is valuable. If the students believe what they are being asked to do or learn is more valuable than the other options they consider available, they will engage in the learning. There are a number of ways that the standard *valuable* can be met.

"PEOPLE APPLY THEMSELVES TO THE EXTENT THEY BELIEVE WHAT THEY ARE DOING IS VALUABLE."

1. The students believe the learning or activity solves a problem they have and/or fulfills a need they have.

2. The students think the learning, or activity in which it is embedded, is interesting or fun.

3. The students experience a sense of "flow" while engaged in the learning or activity. Flow and the research supporting it as a conducive factor in learning is thoroughly presented in the book *Flow: The Psychology of Optimal Experience* by Dr. Mihaly Csikszentmihalyi (Harper Perennial, 1990).

   Flow is that state we enter when the challenges we face and our skill level match "just right." We're not so overly skilled that we become anxious, nor are we so totally under-challenged that we lose interest and disengage. When one is in a state of flow, one loses track of time. Participation in games, sports, and tasks we consider interesting are excellent examples of situations in which we may enter flow.

   We strongly recommend Dr. Csikszentmihalyi's book. We also encourage you to read Dr. Raymond Wlodkowski's book, *Enhancing Adult Motivation to Learn* (Jossey-Bass, 1985) for an excellent development of this concept and many others applicable to this book. *Diversity and Motivation: Culturally Responsive Teaching* (Jossey-Bass, 1995) by Dr. Raymond Wlodkowski and Dr. Margery Ginsberg is another excellent resource we strongly recommend.

STANDARD 2: INVOLVING

This standard is important from two perspectives:

1. people need to feel involved or included in groups in which they are a part, and

2. people tend to apply themselves to the extent they are meaningfully involved in setting directions, determining standards, and/or playing an active role.

There are a number of ways that the standard *involving* needs to be met.

1. The learning *meaningfully involves* the students by having the students:

   - share in the establishment of goals;

   - share in the establishment of ways they can show the required learning; and

   - be involved in processes for developing rubrics/scoring criteria.

2. There are ample opportunities for meaningful choices and decisions by the students.

3. There are ample *opportunities for responses* by each student.

4. The learning/activities *draw from outside knowledge and resources.*

STANDARD 3: SUCCESSFUL

People tend to continue or repeat those things in which they are successful. Feelings of success can come from successfully mastering something or from regular evidence of progress with a complex endeavor. For this standard to be met, the learning/activity must be challenging (but possible) for each student.

Madeline Hunter once defined success as a feeling of forward motion – students do not have feelings of forward motion when the learning is too easy or when it is not possible for them to achieve it.

There are a number of ways the standard *successful* must be met.

1. The students believe the learning/activity is possible for them to do successfully (to high levels of quality).

2. The students believe the learning/activity is challenging.

3. The students obtain evidence of mastery or evidence of progress. (Note: Typically, grades and scores do not provide this evidence. An example of evidence of progress is a chart that dieters keep showing their weekly weights advancing downward to a predetermined goal. Another example is when runners training for a marathon keep charts showing daily and weekly progress with respect to distances and times.)

STANDARD 4: SAFE

Recent brain research tells us that when people do not feel safe there is an actual shift in how the brain functions. The result can be a shut-down in the students' ability to effectively engage in learning processes.

It is a given that the learning environment needs to be such that the students feel safe from any physical danger. However, that's not enough. In addition, the students must feel safe from fear of significant embarrassment.

There are a number of ways the standard *safe* needs to be met. The students must believe they are safe from:

- embarrassment from exposure of anything they consider personally embarrassing with respect to their families, themselves, or their relationships;

- embarrassment from exposure of any significant lack of knowledge or ability;

- a learning/activity that violates their basic beliefs and values; and

- their basic human needs (physical and emotional) not being met.

". . . STUDENTS MUST FEEL SAFE FROM FEAR OF SIGNIFICANT EMBARRASSMENT."

STANDARD 5: CARING

People have a basic need to feel loved, valued, and to have a sense of belonging. The standard *caring* can be met in the following ways:

1. The students feel a *sense of inclusion* (no in/out groups).

2. The students believe that when others are listening to them, the listening is sincere.

3. Praise is specific and accurate, and it is delivered in the manner in which each student wishes.

4. The students have a sense of belonging.

STANDARD 6: ENABLING

Students learn in different ways. If learning needs are not met, students will most likely not meet with success and their motivation for learning will diminish. Therefore, instructional practices must be *enabling* in that they support learning for each student. The standard *enabling* can be met in the following ways:

1. The instructional practices facilitate and do not hinder learning.

2. The learning *builds upon prior knowledge.*

3. The multiple intelligence needs of the students are met.

EXTRINSIC MOTIVATORS HAVE POWERFUL AND OFTEN UNDESIRABLE EFFECTS

Rewards, bribes, acknowledgment, recognition, and celebrations are hot topics in education today. Any discussion of them tends to be emotional and controversial. One reason for this is they have been a part of school for so long it is difficult to objectively look at research and consider new options. Another reason is that change is not only difficult, it is usually approached as "all or nothing," though seldom is "all or nothing" found to be reasonable and do-able.

This section focuses on essential considerations when using rewards, bribes, acknowledgment, recognition, and celebrations. Since each of these terms tends to be defined differently by different people, caution should be taken to focus on concepts and principles and not terms and past practices.

An extrinsic motivator is any act or thing that is openly done for or to someone with the intent of producing a predetermined behavior or change in behavior. Over the years, research has shown us the following with respect to their use:

1. Extrinsic motivators can be very effective in producing behavior or changes in behavior.

2. Extrinsic motivators tend to over-power the effects and existence of intrinsic motivation.

3. Extrinsic motivators increase the students' focus on the extrinsic motivators themselves (points, grades, parties, stickers) while decreasing their focus on desired behaviors.

4. Extrinsic motivators tend to result in lower quality performance and behavior over time.

5. Extrinsic motivators tend to increase predictable, low-risk behaviors while reducing risk taking and complex thinking, creativity, and problem solving.

6. Extrinsic motivators tend to become insufficient over time and require "upping the ante."

7. Extrinsic motivators tend to result in the students returning to their baseline behavior when the motivators are diminished or removed.

8. extrinsic motivators tend to be ineffective in:

    • improving long-term quality performance;

    • promoting self-directed behaviors;

    • developing values such as caring, respect, honesty, and integrity; and

    • promoting self-confidence and intrinsic motivation.

EXTRINSIC MOTIVATORS ACT AS BRIBES

A bribe is an offering to someone in return for a pre-determined behavior or action. Though the word is often used in the context of public and corporate officials, it also represents a common approach used and encouraged over the years in school. Extrinsic motivators (bribes) take many forms. They may be points, grades, rewards, awards, parties, "stickers," notes home, coupons, or money. Extrinsic motivators are actually bribes if:

1. they are known in advance by the students;

2. they are valuable to the students (or promoted as valuable to the students); and

3. they are offered in order to produce a predetermined response or behavior from the students.

Research has shown that when any extrinsic motivator has the above three attributes of bribes, the long-term effects can be less than desirable. Though most of us cringe at the thought of using bribes in school, well-intentioned attempts at recognition and acknowledgment can inadvertently become bribes and rewards that carry associated negative consequences. Compounding the problem, well-intentioned parents may add rewards to your acknowledgment and recognition efforts and thus convert them into bribes or rewards.

EXTRINSIC MOTIVATORS CAN BE USED FOR SHORT-TERM, SINGLE EVENT, PHYSICAL RESPONSES

If you are faced with a situation in which you want an immediate response, and it is unlikely you will get that response any other way, there will probably be little harm if you offer a reward. Be careful, however, to limit these acts to such things as getting help with a physical task for which you will need help only one time. An example of this type of situation is when you need extra-help after school moving equipment and do not expect to need similar help in the future. If you really want help, and the only way to get it is to offer cookies or fruit in return for the work, there probably won't be any harm done if you do. Be certain that:

1. the reward has no effect on grades or evidence of progress with school work;

2. the reward is being offered for a physical (not cognitive or value-oriented) response; and

3. you really have no other option in the situation.

EXERCISE CAUTION IN REDUCING THE USE OF EXTRINSIC MOTIVATORS

Change is difficult for everyone. If your students and their parents are used to extrinsic motivators, and they probably are, be cautious in making changes. One suggestion we can't over emphasize is to never stop doing anything valued by others until you have something else that is successfully "up and running" in their eyes. Announcing sudden changes in reward (or punishment) systems can result in suspicion at best, and outright rebellion at worst.

Take time to develop solid rationale and support for changes. Any existing reward systems need to be left in place until they expire. Operate with dual systems until your new systems are successful and trusted. Provide time and experiences that will help others come along with you.

AVOID THESE CLASSIC DE-MOTIVATORS IN YOUR CLASSROOM

The following are contributors to reduced student intrinsic motivation:

1. the existence of situations in which students feel stupid or embarrassed;

2. insufficient evidence of progress and success;

3. infrequent or vague feedback;

4. coercion and manipulation;

5. competitive situations in which lack of success is probable or feared;

6. sarcasm, put-downs, and criticism;

7. exclusion from decisions regarding goals, means, and standards;

8. insufficient examples and models;

9. insincere listening, recognition, and praise;

10. content and tasks that are perceived to be irrelevant, repetitive, not challenging, or beneath the learners' level;

11. teaching practices that are ineffective or mismatched to the learners' style and multiple intelligence needs;

12. reward systems and bribes;

13. responsibility and accountability without matching authority and autonomy;

14. feelings of exclusion by students;

15. failure of basic needs to be met; and

16. feelings of hopelessness by students.

ENHANCE THE LIKELIHOOD OF INTRINSIC MOTIVATION

Though there is much disagreement as to what promotes or maintains intrinsic motivation, here are a few quick tips that are consistent with the six standards presented earlier.

1. Provide meaningful choices as often as possible while still adhering to rigorous curricular standards.

2. Provide frequent, specific, non-judgmental feedback focused on progress and growth – appropriate acknowledgment and recognition of specific learning behaviors.

3. Embed learning in contextualized activities that the students find enjoyable and worthwhile.

4. Protect each student from embarrassment while holding to high standards and expectations for him/her.

5. Build positive self-concept and high self-esteem through evidence of success provided by challenging and worthwhile tasks.

6. Avoid the use of extrinsic motivators.

7. Use varied and enjoyable instructional activities that match the learning style needs and multiple intelligences of your students. (The focus of the remainder of this book.)

8. Model whatever is to be learned with high levels of enthusiasm.

9. Provide celebrations, including cheers, certificates of mastery, and other exciting, energy and endorphin producing acts. (Be careful, it is possible that while you are not using these as rewards, they may be perceived as rewards by the students or turned into rewarded events by others.)

10. Use effective cooperative learning techniques to promote friendship, bonding, and goal interdependence.

11. Ensure that the learning is challenging but possible for each student.

12. Provide feedback with the five characteristics essential to motivation.

SUMMARY

Motivation is intrinsic. Though extrinsic motivators are powerful, they can either become demotivators in the long-run or they can result in undesirable consequences. Extrinsic motivators are so powerful that they can overpower attempts to manage context and to create a motivating environment.

Develop an environment in which it is most likely students will feel a sense of motivation to learn what is being taught rather than trying to coerce students into learning. To do this requires operating from an understanding of the students' needs.

There are six standards that must be met in a classroom to expect high levels of student motivation. The students must value the learning. They must feel involved in their learning. They must have evidence of success. They need to feel safe from harm and embarrassment. The students must have a sense of belonging, and the instructional practices must promote and not hinder learning.

Extrinsic motivators have been shown through research over the years to have numerous, long-term effects that are considered undesirable by many educators. An extrinsic motivator is defined as anything that has inherent value and is offered (or used as an open or covert threat) to produce or change behaviors.

Much disagreement still exists as to what specifically promotes intrinsic motivation. However, there are general trends that provide guidance in terms of what to do and what to avoid.

CHAPTER 2

ENHANCING MOTIVATION
AND COMMITMENT
TO QUALITY

QUICK TIP

2.1 AFFIRMATIONS & INSPIRATIONS

Display and regularly change affirmations and inspirational quotes and posters. Place them high on the side and back walls of your classroom. This high placement will promote the students being in a visual mode as they see them, and thus facilitate recall. Example affirmations include the following:

- "Don't quit – never give up."
- "The best students in the world pass through this door."
- "I know I can."
- "Try? Try Not. There is only do or not do."   Yoda
- "All of us will succeed."
- "Together we will do it."
- "Learning is essential and fun."
- "Each of us is unique and important."
- "I think, therefore I am."
- "Be the best you can be."
- "Aim high."
- "Practice makes permanent."
- "Expect to succeed"

QUICK TIP

2.2 ATTITUDES ARE CONTAGIOUS

A good friend of ours, Jerry Doyle, is a highly regarded educator who has an attitude from which we can all benefit. Jerry has gone through his career adhering to his pledge,

"I refuse to have a bad day."

In everything that happens, it is possible to choose a positive outlook. Try it. You'll find that the effect on you and the students you work with will be tremendously valuable.

Another good friend of ours once said in a workshop,

"You never tell us we're wrong. No matter what we do, you have a way of validating us. What if we are wrong?"

The answer is simple, though not easy to do. Deliberately design activities to help people continuously improve by building on their strengths. This is done by designing questions and activities that gather information. Use this information to make adjustments in the next activity. With great care and practice, the misperceptions can be gently and effectively corrected.

As teachers we must always ask ourselves,

**"What are we really trying to accomplish?" and
"What is the best, long-term way to achieve it?"**

Another person somewhere once coined the question,

**"Would you rather be right, or would you
rather achieve the results you really want?"**

"IN EVERYTHING THAT HAPPENS, IT IS POSSIBLE TO CHOOSE A POSITIVE OUTLOOK."

2.3   AWESOME TIPS

PURPOSE

To gather focused, specific tips from students that will help them learn.

DESCRIPTION

One of the very best sources for teaching tips is the students. They know what helps them learn – they just may not have the technical language to describe it or the ability to immediately recognize it. All we need to do is frame the questions that will help the students articulate the "quick tips & strategies." The following are some prompts that are successful at gathering useful information, providing we are supportive, caring, non-judgmental, and sincerely interested when we ask them. It is also crucial to be patient. Don't expect everything to come out right away. It takes time to build trust. However, once you start asking – be certain to listen carefully, understand thoroughly, value that a contribution has been made, and honor that contribution.

USES

Motivational Environment

SAMPLE PROMPTS

Think of a time when you were really successful at learning something.

1.   Was someone teaching you?

2.   How was he/she teaching?

3.   What specifically did he/she do?

4.   What kinds of things did he/she say to you?

"IF YOU WERE
TEACHING THIS,
HOW WOULD YOU
DO IT?"

5. Describe the way he/she worked with you?

6. Were you learning with others?

    • How many?

    • What were you doing alike?

    • What were you doing differently?

7. How do you like someone to let you know when you're doing something well?

8. How do you like someone to let you know that you aren't doing something quite right?

9. What has confused you when someone has been teaching you?

10. What has made you angry or too scared when someone has been teaching you?

11. If you were teaching this, how would you do it?

Grade Level: *Elementary, Middle, High School*

Time: *10-20 minutes*

Motivational Standards: *Involving, Caring*

Pluses: *Block Schedules*

QUICK TIP

2.4   BUILDING COMMUNITY THROUGH VENN DIAGRAMS

Ask each student to list everything they can think of about themselves in the following categories:

  • hobbies and interests

  • movies and books they've enjoyed (or types that they enjoy)

  • pets

  • vacations

Ask the students to form pairs or triads – taking care that the students feel safe. Take extreme care to be certain that no one is left out.

Have the groups draw a Venn diagram (or use one provided by you) with a number of circles equal to the number of students in their groups.

Ask the students to record the characteristics they have identified into their Venn diagram in ways that show their similarities and differences. It will probably be necessary to model for the students how to put their similarities in the intersection of the circles and their differences in the

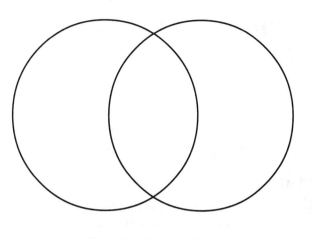

Venn Diagram for Pairs

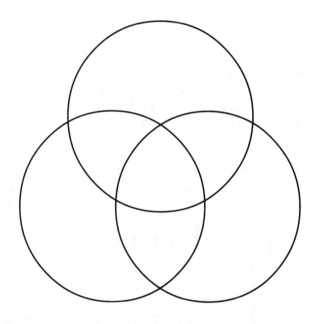

Venn Diagram for Triads

outside portions. After they have finished sharing their list of characteristics, ask them to dig deeper and place several additional characteristics appropriately in the Venn diagram.

Have each group present to the class one characteristic they have in common, and one characteristic for each person that makes him/her unique.

Special thanks to Dr. Raymond Wlodkowski and Dr. Margery Ginsberg for sharing this tip with us.

2.5   CERTIFICATES OF QUALITY PERFORMANCE

PURPOSE

To provide recognition for quality performance and provide viable options for quality performing students.

DESCRIPTION

Just as the scouts have always had badges that are earned for meeting specific criteria, it is helpful to provide such recognition and symbols of achievement in the classroom.

USES

Motivational Environment, Quality

PROCEDURE

1. Develop certificates that are grade level appropriate in appearance. Be certain to provide a place for the student's name, identification of what was done to quality performance levels, and your signature. The principal's signature adds even more significance.

2. Regularly define with the students what would constitute quality level performance with regard to tests, projects, homework, essays, timeliness, etcetera.

3. When a student's performance meets those criteria, he/she is given the certificate of quality performance.

4. If a student's initial effort does not meet the criteria for the certificate, encourage the student to make the necessary refinements until it does.

5. Encourage the students to display their certificates at home. Some teachers even have a place on the certificate for a parent/guardian signature.

6. Occasionally, your teaching may include activities in which some of the higher performing students need not be involved. When that happens, plan an alternative activity to enrich the learning of these higher performers. Use certificates they have earned as "qualifiers" (see page 63) for the special enrichment activity.

HINT

Be careful that these certificates remain symbols of recognition and are not used as extrinsic motivators.

Grade Level: Elementary, Middle, High School

Time: On-going

Special Materials: Printed certificates

Motivational Standards: Successful

Pluses: Block Schedules

Thanks to Veronica Carlson, John Booth, Spence Rogers, and Lori Nau for contributing to this strategy.

2.6 CHECKPOINTS—NOT GOTCHYA'S

Don't grade or score formative assessments. Use them to provide information to yourself and to your students as to the progress being made toward the goal. Consider the analogy of "split times" in a race. The split times are only to provide information, they do not determine the place of the runners at the end of a race. Many a runner has earned an excellent finish with mediocre to poor splits along the way.

QUICK TIP

2.7 CHECK THE MOTIVATIONAL STANDARDS

PURPOSE

To measure the indicators for each motivational standard.

DESCRIPTION

The best way to determine the level at which the standards are being met in a classroom is to combine self-assessment with student assessment of the standards.

USES

Motivational Environment

PROCEDURE

1. Duplicate the motivation questionnaire included with this strategy - making enough copies for each student that will be included in your assessment. If the language in the questionnaire is not at the appropriate level for your students, modify it accordingly.

2. If you are depending on your own responses, put yourself in the place of a typical student in your classroom when developing your responses for each prompt.

3. Ask your students to complete the questionnaire anonymously and honestly. Also ask them to provide the reasons for any responses that are less than positive.

4. Summarize the students' responses. You may wish to compute a numerical average response for each prompt.

5. Consider sharing the response summary with your students. You may find it helpful to engage the students in an open, non-judgmental discussion in order to surface reasons some of the responses were not desirable. If you do this, be sure to listen carefully for what is being said and avoid taking a defensive stance. In the course of

the discussion, be certain to let the students know that you need to work to achieve the established learning goals, but you are willing to accept suggestions that will help with student motivation within that constraint.

It helps to go over the results together as a class. Some students fear being "found out" as not that smart/capable, while others fear criticism and sarcasm from their peers.

Grade Level: Elementary, Middle, High School (all with modifications)

Time: 15 minutes

Special Materials: Copies of motivation survey

Motivational Standards: Involving

Pluses: Block Schedules

TESTING THE MOTIVATIONAL STANDARDS

The following statements describe the feelings and thoughts you may have regarding this class. For each statement, rate its accuracy based on the following scale:

4 – YES! This is absolutely true.

3 – This is really close.

2 – This isn't quite right.

1 – There is some hint of this.

0 – This is absolutely not accurate.

I FEEL SAFE BECAUSE . . .

_____1.   I don't worry about feeling stupid or incapable in this class.

_____2.   Nothing about my friends, family, or myself will be divulged that I may find embarrassing.

_____3.   I'm not labeled or judged in front of others.

_____4.   What happens in class is not displayed or used elsewhere to control me or my behavior.

_____5.   I know I won't be hurt or harmed in any way.

I VALUE WHAT WE'RE LEARNING BECAUSE . . .

_____1.   It's interesting or important to me.

_____2.   It solves a problem that's important to me.

_____3.   Succeeding in this class helps me obtain something I want.

_____4.   I believe what I'm learning is worthwhile and will help me later.

_____5.   It's fun or interesting for me.

I FEEL SUCCESSFUL BECAUSE . . .

_____1.   What I'm learning and what I'm doing is challenging.

_____2.   I know my teacher has confidence in my abilities.

_____3.   I'm expected to achieve at the highest levels, and I'm supported until I do.

_____4.   I believe what I'm doing is worthwhile.

_____5.   I get regular evidence of my progress or mastery.

I FEEL INVOLVED BECAUSE . . .

_____1. I get lots of choices and get to make lots of decisions.

_____2. I have lots of opportunities to engage and respond.

_____3. I'm encouraged to be innovative and creative.

_____4. I'm meaningfully included in establishing goals, procedures, and standards.

_____5. I draw on knowledge and resources from outside school.

I THINK THIS IS A CARING PLACE TO BE BECAUSE . . .

_____1. I feel valued.

_____2. I enjoy being here – it feels good, people care about me and my needs.

_____3. People listen sincerely and supportively to my ideas.

_____4. I feel like I'm a part of the group.

_____5. Praise and recognition are sincere, adequate, and done in ways that are comfortable for me.

IT IS EASY FOR ME TO LEARN BECAUSE . . .

_____1. The instructional practices match my learning style, are effective, and are varied and interesting enough.

_____2. I have a clear understanding of what is expected of me.

_____3. I can see how what I'm learning fits into what I already know.

_____4. I get the help and resources I need to be successful.

_____5. I receive adequate, specific, non-judgmental feedback that's helpful and inspiring.

2.8 CHOICES

People like choices. Deliberately plan your activities so that students have choices. With each activity, build in opportunities for the students to make choices that will not interfere with the main purpose for the activity. For example, if the purpose of an activity is for the students to show their ability to sort things into categories, whether they provide written, oral, or physical evidence may be relevant to our management needs, but isn't relevant to the targeted learning.

QUICK TIP

Example choices that can typically be provided are:

1. Use pen or pencil.
2. Use "black and white" or "color."
3. Word process, type, print or use cursive writing that is neat and large enough for me to read.
4. Present orally or in writing.
5. Draw a picture or use pictures clipped from magazines.

2.9 CLASS COMMITMENTS

PURPOSE

To work with the students to develop agreements governing classroom behavior.

DESCRIPTION

People tend to hit the targets they set for themselves better than those set by others. For that reason, rules governing behavior tend to be more effective when they are established as a collaborative effort. This is a strategy that engages the students in developing rules or guidelines for the classroom.

USES

Motivational Environment, Quality

PROCEDURE

1. Carefully develop 3-5 commitments that you will make to the students.

   Examples:
   - to provide honest, accurate, and supportive feedback on student work;
   - to provide time for working with concepts in class before the students are expected to work with them at home;
   - to never belittle anyone in any manner; and
   - to not ask students to do busy work.

2. In a serious and caring manner share your commitments to the students orally and in writing on a large poster.

3. Ask each student to develop five statements telling what he/she thinks students can do to help improve the quality of his/her learning and the classroom environment.

4. Have them put their ideas on sticky notes with one idea per note.

5. Have the students get into groups of four to five each.

6. Ask the students in each group to share their ideas within their groups.

7. As the students share their ideas within each group, have them stick together those ideas that are similar.

8. Have one group put their sticky note "clumps of ideas" on the wall. Make sure they are spread out with at least 2-3 feet for each idea clump. Have them tell the class what each idea clump is about and what the ideas are in each clump.

9. Have one member of each group take the clumps from his/her group up to the wall and put them with the others — combining with existing clumps and forming new clumps as necessary. Have all the groups do this at the same time.

10. Monitor the groups and help as needed.

11. Quickly facilitate the class in deciding how all the clumps can be combined into 5 to 7 clumps. Make suggestions as needed to keep things moving along rapidly.

12. Ask the groups to work together to determine labels for the clumps. (for example, "Do the best you can on homework and activities.")

13. Ask for a student to volunteer to develop a poster of commitments.

14. Place the poster in a prominent place on a classroom wall.

15. Reflect and process regularly with the students about their successes with the commitments. Students can build portfolios with reflections, testimonials, and other evidence of growth within the commitments.

Commitments

"PEOPLE TEND TO HIT THE TARGETS THEY SET FOR THEMSELVES..."

HINT

Keep this activity going very quickly with no down time.

NOTE: With any activity designed to build a sense of community, be certain the necessary trust levels are in place. For example, most "high-risk" student groups would not initially respond in a desired manner to step 3 in the procedure.

Grade Level: Elementary, Middle, High School

Time: 30 minutes

Special Materials: "Sticky" notes, poster board

Motivational Standards: Involving

Pluses: Group Processing, Block Schedules

Commitments

2.10 CONFLICT RESOLUTION/ PROBLEM SOLVING

PURPOSE

To provide a means by which students can resolve conflicts and seek solutions to their problems.

DESCRIPTION

The 10-step problem solving process presented here is effective for conflict resolution when taught, practiced, and facilitated by a neutral/ trusted third party. The process is also effective for finding solutions to complex problems that are not of a conflict nature.

USES

Motivational Environment

PROCEDURE

1. State the problem in a simple, brief expression. (Example: Students can't agree.)

2. Clarify the problem by identifying all the components or facets of it. This is done by having each person involved (individually) determine the who, what, how, when, and why of the problem. If two students are engaged in what they consider to be a non-resolvable argument, have each one write all he/she can about the problem being certain to address the who, what, how, when, and why.

3. Determine what would be more desirable than what is happening. For example, two arguing students will probably agree that it would be more desirable if they could work together to reach a mutually satisfactory solution. (You may need to help with this step.)

4. Redefine the problem. Just as is done in the judicial system, change the problem into a question. To do this, it is important to address all that has surfaced in the previous steps. In our example, a question might be, "What do we need to do to be able to come to an acceptable agreement?"

5. Identify any constraints on the situation or problem. Before people can resolve a situation, they need to know what the limits are. These may be with respect to rules, basic beliefs, money, or time – just to name a few. In our example, there may not be money necessary for a simple solution, and the school rules probably prohibit a physical fight to determine a winner.

6. Determine who has the ultimate authority to make the decision. It may be the teacher, or it may be the dean of students. It may even be that the whole group will decide by majority rules.

7. Decide how the decision will be made. For example, determine if it

will be done by vote, consensus, or authoritative decision by the teacher, principal, or board of education.

8. Brainstorm and develop multiple solution possibilities. Involve everyone in the process and be certain to adhere to the rules of no judgment. More possible solutions will probably be generated if each person generates possible solutions privately first, and then the group shares and develops more.

9. Evaluate the possible solutions against the constraints, possible impacts, and predetermined desired results.

10. Implement.

Grade Level: Elementary, Middle, High School (all with modifications)

Time: On-going

Special Materials: None

Motivational Standards: Successful, Caring, Involving

2.11 CONNECTIONS - FIND SOMEONE WHO . . .

PURPOSE

To improve the classroom environment for the periodic shifting of groups.

DESCRIPTION

In this strategy the students discover how much they have in common with one another by moving around the room to stand near students who have a certain characteristic like *having a pet.*

This activity, when done quickly and for short intervals, is a lot of fun. It helps students learn about one another and, as a result, they become more comfortable working together. Consequently, rapidly shifting flexible groups function more efficiently and effectively in the classroom.

USES

Motivational Environment

PROCEDURE

1. Instruct the students to move near someone for whom a characteristic you identify is true. Get them started by saying something like, "Move near someone who has a pet dog."

2. Wait patiently while encouraging the students as they begin to discover others who have dogs and form clusters around them.

3. As soon as the students have all moved into groups clustered around someone matching the characteristic, call out another characteristic that will probably connect for one or more students. Be careful that what you pick will not embarrass anyone – the identified characteristic should be very neutral. Example characteristics that work well are, who:

- has a pet	- plays soccer	- likes sardines
- has a cat	- plays piano	- is a student
- enjoys music	- plays chess	- knows ???

VARIATION

Have the students wear signs that represent concepts you have been teaching. Call out characteristics of the concepts and have the students move near someone whose concept has those characteristics.

Grade Level: *Elementary, Middle, High School*

Time: *5-10 minutes*

Special Materials: *None*

Motivational Standards: *Involving, Caring*

Pluses: *Block Schedules, Group Processing, Multiple Intelligences*

QUICK TIP

2.12 CREATIVITY BOOSTERS 9 QUICK TIPS

This tip contains 9 quick tips to boost creativity in the classroom.

1. Have fun and laugh. People learn faster and can think more diversely when they're having fun.

2. Help to remove self-imposed barriers, obstacles, and limitations to students being creative. Discourage phrases, thoughts, and behaviors associated with thoughts of "I can't " or "I don't know how."

3. Never put off students' questions with words, body language, or insincere answers.

4. Give positive recognition to questions you can't answer. Respond with statements like, "That's a really good question," or "You know, I never thought of that before," followed by encouragement to find answers.

5. Model . . .

    • being open to new ideas, perspectives, and assumptions;

    • seeking connections;

    • asking complex questions;

    • challenging assumptions;

    • avoiding what we call phrases like "should have," "would have," and "could have," which we affectionately refer to as "shoulda's, woulda's, coulda's;" and

    • an "I know I can attitude" at all times.

6. Encourage students to question assumptions. Think of all the great discoveries, whether in the arts, historical study, or the sciences. In almost every case the discovery was a direct challenge to existing assumptions at the time.

7. Provide time to think. After giving an assignment involving options or asking an open-ended, complex question, give and insist on think time.

8. Encourage reasonable risk taking - allow/celebrate mistakes. Model and endorse taking reasonable risks to accomplish a goal and, if the risk doesn't work, fix it. Think mistakes, not failures – there is a difference.

9. Encourage students to demonstrate their learning in ways that are exciting and interesting to them – matching their strengths (multiple intelligences). Assess for missing details as needed later.

2.13 CRITERIA FOR CREDIT

PURPOSE

To increase the quality of student work (e.g. homework, notebooks, tests, and projects) through student generated criteria.

DESCRIPTION

At the beginning of each year, most teachers discuss their basic expectations for student work. This strategy uses student generated criteria to increase ownership and the quality of student work.

USES

Motivational Environment, Quality

PROCEDURE

1. Share several examples of excellent and poor homework done by students. Do NOT use examples from students currently in your classroom.

2. Have students study the examples and brainstorm a list of criteria that the "Excellent" papers/examples have in common that the poor ones do not share.

3. Then, help the students develop a list of criteria that the class agrees is important for doing quality homework. Do this by having the students identify the characteristics shared by excellent homework.

4. Display this class list and the examples clearly in the room.

5. In order to be accepted or graded, student work must meet the criteria the class has developed.

VARIATION

The same process can be used to develop criteria for classroom behavior.

Grade Level: Elementary, Middle, High School

Time: 15-30 minutes

Special Materials: Chart paper or poster board, markers, tape

Motivational Standards: Involving, Enabling

Pluses: Block Schedules, Group Processing

Special thanks to John Booth and Spence Rogers for this strategy.

Criteria for Credit

2.14   CURIOSITY WALL

PURPOSE

Provide a fun, non-threatening platform through which the students can seek answers to questions they have regarding specified content or concepts.

DESCRIPTION

Students are naturally curious, but often times their curiosity becomes stifled and they elect not to ask questions. This is unfortunate because curiosity can prove to be a very powerful motivator.

This activity asks students to write one thing they wonder about on a 3 x 5 card, in the form of a question. The students are then given up to a week (based on grade level) to find the answers, record them on their 3 x 5 cards, post them on the "curiosity wall," and prepare to orally share their questions and answers with the class.

In some grade levels and content areas the questions can be from almost any area, because the focus is more on investigation and research. In single discipline areas, you may want to limit the students' questions to your discipline.

USES

Motivational Environment

PROCEDURE

1. Before starting, ask students what the criteria would be for satisfactory answers to their questions. Facilitate the discussion so that criteria such as the following are generated:

    • The source is credible and authoritative, and

    • The answer has enough depth and breadth to meet your needs/curiosity.

2. Only hold the students accountable for the criteria they generate. The purpose of the activity is to generate enthusiasm for the subject.

3. Once a week, provide time for the students to generate their questions.

4. After the allotted time for locating and posting answers, call on five students at random to present their questions and answers. Use the sharing time as an opportunity to probe supportively in order to encourage more questions.

5. Each week, start the activity again and slowly build an extensive "curiosity wall."

HINT

Encourage students to be creative in how they represent their answers and how they share them. Exercise appropriate caution to be certain questions and answers are appropriate for a classroom environment.

Grade Level: *Elementary, Middle, High School*

Time: *5 minutes*

Special Materials: *3 x 5 cards or paper*

Motivational Standards: *Motivational Environment, Valuable, Involving*

Pluses: *Block Schedules, Group Processing, Multiple Intelligences*

2.15   DISPLAY STUDENT WORK

QUICK TIP

Because an audience can have a positive effect on student efforts, find a way to display student work. Whether the work is posted on the wall, published in a student magazine, or performed before an audience, get it out in the open. Several ways this can be done are listed here. For numerous other options select from the products and performances presented in Chapter 7.

- oral presentations
- display walls, tables, and cabinets
- class publications
- photo displays
- open houses and parents' nights

2.16   DON'T BECOME THE ENEMY

QUICK TIP

Avoid using threats and fear tactics. Remember motivation is intrinsic. Tactics like these tend to result in compliance at best and resistance at worst. Instead, seek to create wins. Threats and fear tactics create losers, and losers become more motivated to beat a system than to succeed within it.

QUICK TIP

2.17 EXCITING PREVIEWS

End each class meeting with an exciting preview of the next class. Find at least one thing about the next class that will interest the students and point it out before the students leave. One fun way to do this is to let the students' questions lead into a preview.

2.18 EXPERT CARDS

PURPOSE

To identify students' individual strengths and build self-confidence.

DESCRIPTION

In this strategy, each student creates a "card" depicting one of his/her greatest strengths. The cards are then prominently displayed and referred to when specialized help is needed. This activity is designed as a way to begin identifying the various strengths each student has and building a classroom bank of "experts." This strategy also is a great way to have students learn more about each other, build a sense of community, and feel good about the expertise they bring to the learning situation. It can be done at any age level and in any content.

USES

Motivational Environment

PROCEDURE

1. Have students identify something they do very well, something about which they feel really good, something they feel good enough about to teach someone else. This strength can be something connected with school and a specific content (examples: the ability to add two digit numbers, write a neat paper heading, lead classroom exercises, play the scales), or the strength could be something outside the classroom (examples: the ability to bake delicious cookies, grow beautiful flowers, cut the grass, or entertain children while baby-sitting).

2. Give each student a large index card and ask him to design a "depiction" that represents his personal strength. (The depictions should be the size of an index card.)

3. Give students a chance to work on their depictions. Have colored markers, pens, paper, and any other art supplies that might be helpful.

4. When the students are done, have them share their cards with the class and compare and contrast their strengths and talents.

Expert Cards

5. Once everyone has shared, post the cards on a "Wall of Fame" so students can continue to talk about each other's strengths and also so the cards are easily accessible for future use. The cards can also be posted around the room above the chalkboards like the "A B C" cards.

6. The future use of these cards can take several forms:

    • Writing assignments about student strengths: when they use them, how they learned them, why they developed that particular strength, etcetera.

    • If the strength is a school/content one, the student could help peers when they are having difficulty. This also expands the number of people who can answer questions.

    • Presentations about their strengths.

    • Forming Groups.

Grade Level: Elementary, Middle, High School

Time: 20-30 minutes

Special Materials: Construction paper or 5 x 7 index cards, markers, and tape.

Motivational Standards: Successful, Involving, Caring

Pluses: Block Schedules, Group Processing, Multiple Intelligences

Expert Cards

I am an expert in . . .

_____
Signature

I am an expert in . . .

_____
Signature

2.19   FAVORITE THINGS

PURPOSE

To determine the students' interests in order to facilitate the development of relationships and the formation of connections between the students' interests and the learning.

DESCRIPTION

Use an "Interest Poll" to learn the students' interests. As the school year progresses, whenever the learning can be tied to the students' interests, they will almost naturally care more about it. As students mature, you can expect the types of things that interest them to vary. For example, very young students will care a lot about animals and very little about world issues. It isn't until the late teens that you can expect most of the students to begin gaining interest in global issues.

USES

Ice Breaker, Motivational Environment

PROCEDURE

Ask the students to answer questions like the following, but be careful to provide students with the opportunity to not answer if they choose.

- What's your favorite story/novel?

- What's your favorite TV show?

- What movies have you really enjoyed?

- What are your hobbies?

- A really important goal I have is . . .

- This year, I would like to learn . . .

- The thing I would like to do more of is . . .

- My favorite pet is/would be . . .

Grade Level: *Elementary, Middle, High School*

Time: *Variable*

Special Materials: *None*

Motivational Standards: *Valuable, Involving*

Pluses: *Block Schedules, Multiple Intelligences*

2.20 FEEDBACK STRATEGIES

12 IMPORTANT WAYS TO IMPROVE STUDENT PERFORMANCE

PURPOSE

To provide students with the feedback that is an essential part of the learning process.

DESCRIPTION

Feedback is a crucial part of the instructional process. It's how we gain the evidence of progress or mastery that we need as learners. It's also how we learn what we're doing well and what improvements need to be made.

How feedback is given has a tremendous effect on the learners' abilities to use it and/or their level of motivation. What follows are numerous tips for improving the effectiveness of feedback in your classroom.

USES

Motivational Environment

FEEDBACK TIPS

1. *Non-judgmental Feedback*

   Help to maintain each student's dignity by providing non-judgmental feedback. Avoid negative and positive judgments and try to use neutral recognition of contributions such as:

   - "Thanks."
   - "Thank you for contributing."
   - "I see what you mean by that."
   - "Let me see if I understand . . ."
   - "I understand what you mean."
   - "Okay, and ..." (using the same phrase as you receive contributions from numerous students.)

   Also try specific recognition of the expected behavior or performance standard, such as:

   - "I see that you correctly selected linear as a sampling pattern. Now work on when to apply random and clustered patterns."

- "That's an appropriate font and point size for your visuals; everyone in the room can read them easily."

- "The colors you've selected match what we've learned about visibility, consistency, and learners' needs."

2. Scores, Numbers, Letters, and Levels as Feedback

Dieters and runners often record or chart their progress as a way of monitoring themselves. Showing progress can contribute a motivating effect. Seeing improvement can be highly motivating, but if care isn't taken, seeing backsliding or stagnant data can be discouraging. Therefore, design progress charts so that meaningful progress without lowered standards is almost certain. Normal and minor backslides tend not to show. For example, some dieters and athletes chart their progress weekly rather than daily. Sometimes they chart their daily progress in pencil and use bright colors for the weekly data.

SHOWING PROGRESS
CAN CONTRIBUTE A
MOTIVATING EFFECT

Be certain to chart data that truly shows progress. Notice that dieters do not chart "grades" to indicate how well they did – they chart the actual *impact* data such as number of calories consumed, daily or weekly weight in pounds or kilograms. (Also note, for exercise programs, people may chart distances run, times for distances run, pounds lifted, or number or repetitions). In school our tendency has been to depend on grades to provide this evidence – don't. Record grades in your grade book, but also help students track the objectives they've learned, speed at which they can do something, or some other specific data showing intended progress against established performance standards.

3. Qualitative Feedback

This is the feedback that tends to be really motivating. Dieters experience this through feedback such as discovering they fit into old clothes, feeling more energetic, having fewer aches and pains, and being able to wear clothes or styles that they've always wanted to. Students can enjoy this same type of feedback through comments such as:

- "This set of directions you wrote was very easy to follow. One, two, three, and I was done."

- "Your visuals with this presentation could be read by the students in the back of the room because you used dark colors and very large, neat printing."

- "Your arguments get tighter and tighter and, at the same time, easier to follow."

4. Specific, Diagnostic Feedback

This type of feedback is very helpful when students are new to a skill and are open to guiding feedback. It is also helpful when students are anxious to know what they need to do to quickly solve a problem. An example: "When you hold a computer key down for more than one second, the computer will automatically begin repeating whatever letter that key represents until you release the key. If you don't want a letter to repeat, be certain to let the key up in less than a second."

Be certain to provide an opportunity for the student to practice the corrected behavior before too much time passes.

5. Feedback Designed to Cause Dissonance

Take extreme care to use compassion. Feedback can always hurt even if it's labeled constructive, positive, or supportive. We have even heard it said that the labels constructive, positive, and supportive for feedback are labels used to help the giver of the feedback feel okay, while the feedback may still be perceived by the receiver as destructive, negative, or under-cutting.

In many situations, specific and non-judgmental feedback will provide adequate information. When it is essential to point out what is wrong, be certain that your positive intentions are made clear through the positive and supportive feedback that you provide. Also, separate the target of the feedback from the person.

Be careful of using words like "but" or "however" when providing feedback. Students quickly learn that when positive or non-judgmental feedback is followed by words like but and however, the real issue is whatever follows. Soon, our students learn to tune out until they hear these *magic words* that tell them the real truth is coming. For many people, the word **BUT** has actually become an acronym for "**B**ehold, the **U**nderlying **T**ruth."

6. Praise and Recognition Feedback

Everyone enjoys recognition for what he/she has done well. There are lots of ways of meeting this need, but be cautious. Praise should be sincere and specific. Students quickly learn when praise isn't sincere or is empty. Avoid effusive or false praise. Be careful of appearing insincere or not authentic.

Ask each student how he/she likes to receive praise or recognition, and then take care to provide it in that way. Some students like praise and recognition to be public; some prefer it private. Some want their parents informed, and some want it kept for themselves. Provide a safe way for the students to tell you how they want praise and recognition, and then honor their wishes.

7. *Growth Feedback*

Effective feedback tends to have positive effects on learning and motivation. Therefore, it is important to pick the focus of your energy wisely. Focus feedback toward growth. Almost everyone can experience growth, so this provides an opportunity for positive, supportive feedback even when students are having difficulty with mastery. A focus on growth also helps to create a mindset of continuous improvement.

8. *Constructive Criticism*

Constructive criticism may be appropriate in situations in which safety, time, or costs are a primary concern. It may also be appropriate when the students request it.

When providing constructive criticism, be certain to address the needs of the students. In addition, the criticism needs to be informative, immediate, matched to performance standards, instructive, and recognizing of the student's efforts and intentions. Be certain to provide time and support for the student to do correctly whatever he/she is to be doing, and then to practice the correct behavior.

9. *Tone*

Feedback needs to be supportive, constructive, and caring—never condescending, attacking, or negative. Also avoid false praise or flattery, and be careful to provide feedback in ways that are comfortable for the students.

10. *Timing and Frequency*

The timing for feedback is important. Sometimes feedback is more effective if there is time for self-reflection or more opportunities and experience. Sometimes learners are in a state of low self-confidence and immediate feedback can have a negative effect.

The appropriate frequency for feedback varies based on the developmental level of the learner with the given task or situation. Typically, frequent feedback is important in the early learning stages in order to develop skills and/or confidence.

11. *Self-Assessment Feedback*

With adequate rubrics that are well understood by the students, self-assessment is a wonderful source of effective feedback. Periodic peer, parent/guardian, and/or teacher assessments with the same rubrics help to ensure accurate and high quality self-assessment and feedback practices by the students.

12. Positive Feedback

Draw attention to what's right.

Whenever possible, indicate to students what they have done well rather than what they have done poorly. Through pointing out what's right, we provide the same information as if we pointed out what's wrong. The difference is in how it's received and the energy that will then be focused on growth and improvement, rather than on frustration or anger.

Grade Level: Elementary, Middle, High School

Time: On-going

Motivational Standards: Safe, Successful, Caring, Enabling

2.21 GOAL ACTION PLANS

PURPOSE

To promote a goal orientation and commitment to a vision.

DESCRIPTION

This strategy improves student motivation and the quality of work because it involves them in the development of a vision for themselves and a clear plan for achieving it.

USES

Motivational Environment, Quality

PROCEDURE

1. Before beginning this strategy with your students, complete long-term and short-term goal action plans for yourself. Present your examples to the students while describing how they will help you achieve your goals.

2. Provide each student with two cards that are at least 5 x 7. If cards are not available, they can use paper.

3. Ask the students to reflect over goals they may have. Provide examples like going to college, earning the money to buy a car, saving enough money to purchase a gift, or doing well on a science project. Help the students distinguish between long-term goals and short-term goals.

4. Have each student select one long-term and one short-term goal for

himself/herself. Ask the students to write their long-term goals on the top of one of their cards, and their short-term goals on top of their other card.

5. Describe and model how to determine the essential steps (the action plan) that need to be completed to achieve a goal. Let them see how you did this with your goal action plans.

6. Ask the students to record the essential steps for each of their goals under the corresponding goals. Also ask them to record the date or dates by which they will complete each step.

7. Have the students keep their goal action plans in a safe place. Weekly, ask the students to monitor their progress and adjust their plans as needed.

Grade Level: Elementary, Middle, High School

Time: 40 minutes

Special Materials: 5 x 7 cards

Motivational Standards: Involving, Valuable, Successful

Pluses: Block Schedules

2.22 GOAL TREES

PURPOSE

To provide an active and visual approach to learning goals.

DESCRIPTION

Learning is certainly enhanced by striving to learn something we have wondered about. This strategy is designed to take advantage of this natural curiosity by providing a visual model that shows the students the attainment of their learning goals. This is accomplished through the metaphor of a tree which grows leaves (learning goals) which fall to the ground after they've reached their peak (been fulfilled) and are then replaced by new leaves (new learning goals that can only be understood because the first goals were achieved).

USES

Motivational Environment

PROCEDURE

1. On a very large sheet of paper draw a large tree that looks similar to a tree in winter.

2. Lead a discussion with the students about the major topic(s) and concept(s) of the unit you are about to begin.

3. Ask them individually or in groups to pause to wonder about the topics/concepts in order to develop learning goals – things they wonder about and would like to know.

4. Have them write these goals on removable "sticky" notes and put them on the tree as leaves. (If developmentally appropriate, do the writing for the students, including drawings for clarification.)

5. Check the removable "sticky" note "LEAVES" in order to make certain that you can adjust the unit so that the students will be able to pursue their learning goals as a part of the unit.

6. Periodically throughout the unit, provide time for the students to reflect on their goals. When they feel they have met a goal, ask them to put it on the ground beneath the tree and replace it with a new goal.

7. At the end of the unit, provide a forum for the students to share their goals and discoveries.

NOTE

Using the tree and the sticky note leaves is just a way to make an abstract concept like goals more tangible for students. If you have another way of accomplishing this that you feel is more developmentally appropriate, we encourage you to use it.

VARIATION

Goal Wall

Grade Level: Elementary, Middle, High School

Time: 20 minutes

Special Materials: Outline of a tree on bulletin board, or prepared Goal Wall area, and self-stick removable notes.

Motivational Standards: Involving

Pluses: Block Schedules, Multiple Intelligences

2.23 GOLD CARDS

PURPOSE

To encourage and support students becoming more self-directed and responsible.

DESCRIPTION

A Gold Card is to a student in a classroom much like a driver's license is to a potential driver. It is a tangible symbol which certifies that specific, responsible behaviors have been demonstrated by someone, and thus that person (student) is licensed (trusted) to do certain things.

Students acquire Gold Cards when they demonstrate to their teachers, at times of their choosing, that they meet all specified criteria. (Refer to the Gold Card Status Student Assessment Form included with this strategy.) It is each student's responsibility to seek out the teacher when he/she is ready to provide evidence that he/she meets the criteria. Students with Gold Cards are those students who have demonstrated an ability to make decisions responsibly and to be more responsible for their own conduct. Possession of a Gold Card means the student can say, "I am responsible. I am trusted. I exhibit positive behaviors a majority of the time. I can handle making more choices. I am licensed to make choices and accept responsibilities identified on my Gold Card."

Gold Cards should not be used as rewards for good behavior. Nor should the lack of a card be considered a punishment. This strategy is designed to promote self-evaluation of responsible behaviors and to match responsibilities given to responsibility shown. (See chapter one.)

USES

Motivating Environment, Quality

GOLD CARD
Criteria Met By

_____
Student

_____
Teacher

_____
Date

PROCEDURE

1. Prepare Gold Cards.

2. Determine, preferably with student input, the behavioral standards that should be met if a student is to have earned choices such as going to the library or restroom unaccompanied or using the computers unattended. A sample Gold Card Status Student Assessment Form (included with this strategy) can be used to record the positive behaviors.

3. Determine the Gold Choices that are appropriate for those students who show responsible behaviors.

4. Model targeted behaviors up front.

5. Do a lot of goal setting with the students at the beginning of the year for at least 4-6 weeks.

6. Have students self-assess with the targeted behaviors in their journals.

7. Explain to the students how they may meet with you whenever they are ready to show how they have consistently demonstrated the Gold Card behaviors and thus have earned a card.

8. As individual students apply and show you how they meet the standards for a Gold Card, present them with a card and its associated choices.

9. Students may be taken off Gold Card status or request that they be taken off.

VARIATION

Name the cards after the school color (e.g. Blue Cards, Green Cards)

Grade Level: Elementary, Middle

Time: On-going

Special Materials: None

Motivational Standards: Involving, Successful

Many thanks to the Greenland Elementary School 5/6 team (who uses "Green Cards" after the school colors) for introducing us to this strategy. They asked that readers be advised NOT to use these cards as either rewards or punishments.

Gold Card Status
Student Assessment Form

Name_____ Date _____

C = Consistently   M = Most of the Time   S = Sometimes   R = Rarely

POSITIVE BEHAVIOR	C	M	S	R
Response to Peers				
Allows others to learn and enjoy school				
Ignores/discourages negative peer behavior				
Works cooperatively with others				
Respects personal space and property				
Speaks politely to all				
Personal Responsibility for Learning				
Works well independently				
Participates in class activities/discussions				
Pays attention in class				
Assumes responsibility for assigned work				
Organizes materials and belongings; prepares as directed				
Response to Adults				
Allows adults to do their jobs				
Accepts suggestions and redirection				
Speaks politely to all				
Responds immediately to adult directives				
Response to School Rules				
Demonstrates self-control in and out of the classroom (bathroom, hallways, cafeteria, playground, etc.)				
Is fair and follows rules on playground (on equipment, in games, language used)				
Shares school-owned equipment				
Demonstrates self-control in novel/non-routine situations (field trips, assemblies, substitute teachers, guests, etc.)				

"Consistently" or "Most of the Time" ratings are required on all items of positive behavior for Gold Card status.

Meets criteria for Gold Card status   ☐ Yes   ☐ No

If "No," describe a plan of action to meet criteria for Gold Card status.

GOLD CARD
Criteria Met By

_____
Student

_____
Teacher

_____
Date

GOLD CARD
Criteria Met By

_____
Student

_____
Teacher

_____
Date

GOLD CARD
Criteria Met By

_____
Student

_____
Teacher

_____
Date

GOLD CARD
Criteria Met By

_____
Student

_____
Teacher

_____
Date

GOLD CARD
Criteria Met By

_____
Student

_____
Teacher

_____
Date

GOLD CARD
Criteria Met By

_____
Student

_____
Teacher

_____
Date

GOLD CARD
Criteria Met By

_____
Student

_____
Teacher

_____
Date

GOLD CARD
Criteria Met By

_____
Student

_____
Teacher

_____
Date

2.24 HIGH EXPECTATIONS

As you or the students track grades, initally record a perfect score for every grade that can be improved or needs to be done. This way the students can see how good a grade they can earn by completing everything well.

QUICK TIP

2.25 ICE BREAKER - ALPHABET SOUP

PROCEDURE

Ask everyone to take turns stating his/her name and to follow it with a statement of something he/she likes to do that begins with the first letter of his/her name.

Examples:

"My name is Shawna, and I live to skate!"

"My name is Jason, and I enjoy jogging in Central Park before school."

"My name is Bart, and I look forward to spending my summer vacation boating with my family and friends."

Time: 10 minutes

2.26 ICE BREAKER - SPIDER WEB

PROCEDURE

1. Begin the activity by stating your name and something interesting about yourself. (e.g., "My name is Miss Grass, and I would like to be a member of the U.S. Olympic Gymnastics Team.") Then, while holding onto the end of a ball of yarn, toss the ball to someone else in the room.

2. Continue the process until all have shared and a spider web pattern has been created.

3. Reverse the process by repeating the name and the interesting thing for the person who tossed you the yarn, tossing the ball back to him/her. Wind the slack as you progress.

Time: 10-15 minutes

2.27   ICE BREAKER - I'D LIKE TO INTRODUCE . . .

PROCEDURE

1. Initially have students get into pairs, exchange names, and share something interesting about themselves.
2. Then, have each pair meet with another pair and introduce their partners. (The introductions need to include the name and interesting things of each partner.)
3. Then, four meet four and make introductions.
4. Then eight meet eight with proper introductions given.

Time: 15 minutes

2.28   ICE BREAKER - WHO'S WHO?

PROCEDURE

1. Give each student a 3 x 5 card and have him/her write five adjectives which best describes who he/she is.
2. Collect cards, shuffle them, and pass out the cards to the students.
3. Each person then reads the card he/she has been dealt and attempts to identify the student being described.
4. When all cards have been read, students indicate whether or not they were correctly matched.
5. At the conclusion of the activity, it is fun to paste the student's school picture on the card and put all the cards on the bulletin board so students can read the cards at their leisure and begin making connections with their classmates.

CAUTION

Students must know and adhere to accepted procedures for interacting with each other prior to doing this activity.

Time: 10 minutes

2.29 ICE BREAKER - STUDENT OF THE WEEK

PROCEDURE

1. At the beginning of the school year, give each student a 5 x 7 card. Have them write their names on the card and responses to the following items:

    • Number of members in family

    • Number of siblings and ages

    • Favorite:

- Food	- Hobbies
- Type of music	- Special interests
- Types of movie	- School subjects
& TV shows	- Recreational activities
- Book	

2. Collect these cards and select one at random each week. The student selected will be the featured "Student of the Week."

3. Throughout the week, share with the class the information the student has given. This is also a great time to allow the student to do something "special" if it is appropriate. (e.g., be first in line if the class is going somewhere, select a day to not turn in a daily assignment, etc.)

CAUTION

Be certain that students are not asked to share anything they may find embarrassing. Also, check for appropriateness of responses.

Time: 5-10 minutes

2.30 INTERESTING STARTS

Start any phase of your lessons with phrases that are true and of the type that tend to attract people's attention. The following are several examples:

Use numbers: "There are 3 reasons that ..."

Use challenges: "I wonder how many of us can ..."

Use fun: "It's more fun if ..."

Use focusers: "The one, most important cause is ..."

Use questions that connect us: "How many of us have had this problem ...?"

QUICK TIP

QUICK TIP

2.31   INVITING LANGUAGE

Exercise care to use language that is inviting and non-coercive. For example try, "I'd like to invite you to . . ."

Thanks to Dr. Margery Ginsberg and Dr. Raymond Wlodkowski for this tip.

2.32   MEMORY WALL

PURPOSE

To create feelings of progress, inclusion, and belonging.

DESCRIPTION

Create a memory wall loaded with pictures of students engaged in learning throughout the year. Just about everyone likes to see pictures of himself/herself – particularly if the pictures show growth, accomplishment, or involvement.

USES

Motivational Environment

PROCEDURE

1. Be certain that you get a relatively equal number of pictures of each student each time you add to the wall.
2. Do not use pictures that capture students in poses they may consider embarrassing.
3. Obtain permission from each student before you display pictures of him or her.
4. Photograph a lot of different group activities. These pictures will provide reminders of success and progress.
5. At the end of the year, put all the pictures in a scrapbook, label it well, and keep it in a special place in your classroom.

Grade Level: *Elementary, Middle, High School*

Time: *On-going*

Motivational Standards: *Safe, Valuable, Involving, Caring*

Pluses: *Block Schedules*

2.33 MONITORING STUDENT ATTITUDES REGARDING INSTRUCTIONAL APPROACHES

QUICK TIP

When teaching strategies and pace do not meet the learning style needs of the learners, the effects can be less than desirable. Students may lose interest or become frustrated. In either case, they may soon "check out." One quick way to check for the impact of instructional approaches is to provide a quick survey such as the following:

Circle each word that indicates your feelings about

this class/strategy/project.

Interesting	Scary	Too hot
Too fast	Frustrating	Too cold
Boring	Practical	Enjoyable
Fun	Stimulating	Too hard
Challenging	Useful	Too easy
Exciting	Relevant	Takes too much time
Usable	I feel valued	Need more time to do well
Feels right	I'm glad I'm here	
Ho hum	Stupid	Makes me feel stupid
Just the right pace	It's not your fault	I like it

Circle each word that indicates your feelings about

this class/strategy/project.

Interesting	Scary	Too hot
Too fast	Frustrating	Too cold
Boring	Practical	Enjoyable
Fun	Stimulating	Too hard
Challenging	Useful	Too easy
Exciting	Relevant	Takes too much time
Usable	I feel valued	Need more time to do well
Feels right	I'm glad I'm here	Makes me feel stupid
Ho hum	Stupid	
Just the right pace	It's not your fault	I like it

2.34 MOTIVATING CHALLENGES

Many of us find challenging situations quite motivating. We can use this whenever we want students to generate ideas, recall facts, or brainstorm. Several examples to show how this is done are as follows:

QUICK TIP

- There are several states that are well known for recreation provided by lakes, rivers, and sea shores. Let's see how many each group can come up with.

- I'm thinking of three ways praise can be given that could cause harm. Work together to determine all the ways you can agree that praise can actually be ineffective or hurtful. Let's see if your groups can come up with the same three I'm aware of.

- Let's see which group can think of the most different ways wood is used by humans.

2.35 MOTIVATING LESSONS

PURPOSE

To assist teachers in designing units that are most likely motivating to students.

DESCRIPTION

Students tend to work on those things they find interesting or that meet a need they have. Unfortunately, what the students want is not always what must be taught. The following strategy blends the personal and the educational needs in such a way that increased motivation and learning benefits all.

USES

Motivating lesson design

PROCEDURE

1. Draw a "T" chart.
2. Label the left side, "What the students need" (to learn).
3. Label the right side, "What the students want" (to learn or have happen in class).
4. In the "What students need" section, identify each of the following that is appropriate for the impending unit.

What the Students Need:	What the Students Want:

    A. The information students need to learn and how it will be tested.

    B. The conceptual understandings students need to gain and how it will be tested.

    C. The content skills students need to acquire and how they will be checked.

    D. The higher level processes students need to develop and how they will be checked.

5. In the "What the students want" column, list all that you know regarding what the students want as part of the unit. (Asking the students is very helpful. Most likely they will say, "have fun and be involved/active" in addition to content interests.)

6. Use the data in your "T-Chart" to plan your unit.

NOTE

For each appropriate "want," identify how it will be built into the unit and how you will let the students know it's coming. It is important to address students' "wants" early or they will tend to lose interest.

Grade Level: Elementary, Middle, High School

Time: N/A

Special Materials: None

Motivational Standards: N/A

Pluses: Block Schedules, Group Processing

What the Students Need:	What the Students Want:

QUICK TIP

2.36   NUMBERS MOTIVATE

For some reason people perk up when they hear numbers. This can be used to focus students' attention on major points. For example, rather than saying there are several things we need to do today, say, "there are three things we need to do today." Then number them as you go over them with the class. Also, in order to help more students, be sure that the three things are said, written and, if it makes sense, that visible models or pictures are provided.

2.37   PERSONAL POSTER

PURPOSE

To establish the base for a high quality, collaborative classroom.

DESCRIPTION

This strategy results in the teacher and students creating and sharing Personal Posters to introduce themselves to the class. (The content of the poster can focus on family, important dates, accomplishments, likes and dislikes, goals, hobbies, etcetera.) This activity can be completed in class, taking 1 to 2 hours; or introduced on one day with home-time given for development, taking 2 to 3 days. An added benefit of this activity is that it can be used to facilitate getting acquainted in a new learning environment.

USES

Motivational Environment, Quality

PROCEDURE

1. Create and share your personal poster and at least two others done in different styles. Be certain all examples represent desired standards for high quality work.

2. Help the class generate common criteria for quality as seen in the three models.

3. Have the students create their own personal posters, adhering to the quality criteria identified by the class.

4. Have the students share their posters with the entire class and display them in the classroom for a determined length of time.

VARIATION

Following the same format above, students design:

- Hats or T-shirts;
- A product based on a goal;
- School motto, or relevant theme; or
- Name Strips and/or Vanity Plates. (After the strips are designed and shared, they can be posted around the room or used as name plates on desks until everyone knows each other.)

NOTE

Remind students that whatever they do/present in school needs to be appropriate for a school setting. Also, be certain that whatever the students share of a personal nature has the approval of their family or guardians.

EXTENSION

As students share their posters, other students reflect on connections, jot them on "sticky" notes, and put the notes on the posters when they are displayed.

Grade Level: Elementary, Middle, High School

Time: 30 minutes to 2-3 days - varies with scope

Special Materials: Chart paper, markers

Motivational Standards: Involving, Caring, Successful

Pluses: Block Schedules, Multiple Intelligences

Special thanks to Shari Graham for this strategy.

2.38   PERSONALLY CONNECT

After throwing out a question to the class, make eye contact with everyone before calling on a volunteer.

QUICK TIP

2.39   PRAISE THAT'S NON-JUDGMENTAL

Give non-judgmental praise by factually pointing out what specific, desired characteristics are present in a given situation. (e.g., "I see you have your book out and ready at the beginning of class.")

2.40   PRAISE WITH SENSITIVITY

Not all people are comfortable receiving praise and yet others thrive on it. Some people like praise out in the open, but some people prefer it to be private. Many people actually resent praise if it is embarrassing or considered to be insincere. Be certain to praise students when they deserve it. Here are a couple tips for using praise effectively.

- Give praise the way the student likes to receive it, whether that's openly or in private. A rule of thumb is that praise is safest when it's one-on-one.

- Only give praise that is sincere.

2.41   PROTECT STUDENTS FROM THEIR GREATEST FEARS

From the beginning, through everything you do, ensure and prove to the students that their greatest fears will not come true. Introduce the year or class by letting them know up front that the following 5 statements are true, and do all that is possible to prove it as the year progresses.

1. No one will be embarrassed.
2. Class will be interesting, fun, and worthwhile.
3. You are competent, and they will succeed as others have before them.
4. You are fair and honest.
5. You have integrity and will follow through on your commitments.

Adapted from *Limitless Learning: Making Powerful Learning an Everyday Event* (1996, Zephyr Press). Thanks to the author Doug McPhee.

2.42 PROVIDE MEANINGFUL CHOICES

People have a basic need to feel free and independent (Dr. William Glasser). When students begin to feel this need is not being met, the result can be a loss of motivation to learn. Therefore, whenever possible and appropriate, give students the opportunity to make meaningful choices. Opportunities for student choices include the following:

- the type of writing instrument they will use for assignments;

- the learning or practice activity they will complete (providing the options meet the expected objectives);

- how to implement classroom procedures;

- how information will be conveyed in assignments (orally, in writing, by picture, etcetera); and

- when appropriate, the order or time in which assignments will be completed.

When students cannot be given choices, be certain to have sound rationale for why not. If they have been given enough opportunities for meaningful choices along the way, they are much more likely to be satisfied with reasonable rationale for not having a choice.

QUICK TIP

2.43 PURPOSE DRIVEN

Be certain the students know the purpose for whatever is being learned and done. This is important for individual efforts, but it is even more true with cooperative groups because it helps to unify the group based on a common purpose.

QUICK TIP

2.44 QUALIFIERS

PURPOSE

To increase the importance of homework and other assignments in the classroom, as well as increase the quality of the work received.

DESCRIPTION

"Qualifiers" are those assignments/tasks that must be completed by students to be "qualified" to take a test or retest. For those teachers who use retesting as part of their assessment of students, the idea of using homework as a qualifier has helped with the preparedness of the students at test or retest time.

USES

Quality

PROCEDURE

1. Share with students the value of homework or practice for achieving success in almost anything that is skill oriented.

2. Explain the concept of qualifiers in "outside of school" contexts.

3. Explain to the students that in order to test or retest, the qualifiers (homework) must be completed. Adhere to the agreed upon "Criteria for Credit." (See Criteria for Credit strategy.)

4. When the "qualifier" is done to the expected quality levels, check it off as done.

VARIATIONS

This idea works well when used along with "Criteria for Credit."

Grade Level: Elementary, Middle, High School

Time: On-going

Special Materials: None

Motivational Standards: Successful

Pluses: Block Schedules

2.45   QUALITY ASSIGNMENTS

QUICK TIP

Post on the bulletin board several samples of assignments that are done in high quality ways. Be sure to include diverse examples.

Group the assignments around a circle or a square in which you have written the characteristics of the examples that make them quality. Typical characteristics include: neat, organized, well labeled, complete, or finished after gaining help. (See "Criteria for Credit" for a similar approach that provides for more student involvement.)

Whenever student work is not up to standards, ask them to compare their work to the quality examples, determine what refinements need to be made, and make them. Caution: DO NOT use examples from students known to your students. Variation: Ask the students to determine the characteristics the excellent examples have in common. (See "Quick Rubrics that Foster Commitment.")

2.46 QUICK RUBRICS THAT FOSTER COMMITMENT

PURPOSE

To involve students in the development of the standards for specific tasks.

DESCRIPTION

People tend to apply themselves to the extent that they value and are involved in whatever is being done. This is a quick strategy that can be used to engage the students in the development of the standards for a given task. The result of doing this is typically increased understanding of and commitment to meeting the standards. Use this strategy whenever one level of expectations is sufficient – good enough or not good enough.

This strategy is very effective when . . .

1. what is being analyzed to develop standards is not overly complex;

2. the standards to be developed are quite holistic; and/or

3. only one aspect of a complex task is to be addressed at a time.

This rubric development strategy can be very effective with:

- homework assignments (general appearance and quality)

- visuals for an oral presentation

- eye contact in a presentatio

- clarity of descriptions and

- theme in an original short story.

USES

Motivational Environment, Quality

PROCEDURE

1. Ask the students to work in groups of three to five.
2. Duplicate for the groups a three circle Venn diagram. The Venn diagram should fill a sheet of standard notebook paper.
3. Provide the students with three examples of what you consider to be exemplary work for the given task. (This works even better if the students are able to locate and obtain the exemplary examples.)
4. Ask the students to label each of the 3 circles of their Venn diagrams with the label being used for each of the three exemplary examples.

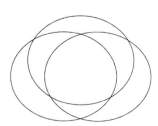

5. Have the students identify the significant qualitative and/or quantitative characteristics for each exemplary example (called an exemplar) and put them in the Venn diagram appropriately. The primary objective here is for the students to identify the *quality characteristics* that the three exemplars have in common.

6. Have the groups share their common quality characteristics while you, or a designated student, records them on the overhead or on a sheet of butcher paper.

7. Combine, separate, and/or refine as necessary for accuracy, precision, thoroughness, and clarity. The result is a set of agreed upon standards (criteria) for the given task.

8. Have a student (or group of students) create a nice poster with the standards. For each standard, there needs to be at least one clarifying example. (These clarifying examples are called anchors because they anchor the descriptive phrases to examples that are concrete.)

9. Prominently display the poster with its "anchors" so your students can refer to it as needed.

10. Have students self and peer assess against these standards.

HINT:

If these standards are being used for a task that is to be graded, let these standards qualify a student's work for a "B." Anything better than the standards earns an "A," and anything short of the standards isn't done yet.

Grade Level: Elementary, Middle, High School (all with modifications)

Time: 20 minutes

Special Materials: Venn Diagrams

Motivational Standards: Involving, Enabling, Successful

Pluses: Block Schedules, Group Processing, Multiple Intelligences

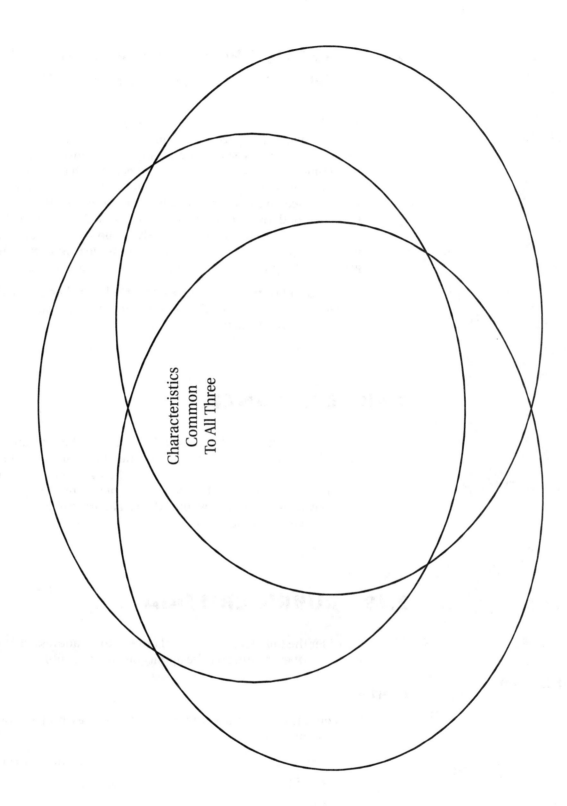

Characteristics
Common
To All Three

2.47 REDUCE PUT-DOWNS & SARCASM THROUGH STUDENT INPUT

There is no place for sarcasm in a classroom! Take time to engage the students in group discussions about the effects of put-downs and sarcasm. This can be started by asking the students to individually recall times when they've been the targets of such behavior. Ask them to record their feeling on sheets of paper anonymously. You can then read their feelings to the class, or have students pass them and read them out loud. (Be certain the students know ahead of time that their responses will be shared anonymously.) Follow-up by either leading a whole group discussion, or use a cooperative learning structure to generate a no put-down policy and ways to make it work.

Don't expect fast miracles. It takes time to change behaviors. Help the students to practice providing non-judgmental and specific feedback. In the long-run, it will payoff.

2.48 RELEVANCE

Be certain the students know how they can use what you are teaching them. The more mature the students, the more important it is to them to see a value or a need for what they are being expected to learn. The need may simply be that they don't want their parents to ground them, or, it may be they know they must do well in order to get into college or get a particular job they want.

2.49 RUBRIC CRITERIA

Consider the following as essential criteria to be addressed in student rubrics. Not everything will be applicable in every rubric.

CONTENT

The content shown in the students' performances, projects, or processes should be …

- accurate
- valid
- relevant
- precise
- supported/justified

- adequate in depth and breadth
- logical
- clear
- correct

- insightful
- apt
- focused
- thorough

FORM

The form used by the students should show effective . . .

- organization
- adherence to focus
- style
- sequence
- mechanics/usage

IMPACT

The students' work should produce a desired impact as shown by their work being . . .

- resolving of an issue
- satisfying
- persuasive
- interesting
- convincing
- engaging
- moving
- winning
- informing
- a successful application of an important skill or concept

PROCESS

The students' work should show processes that are . . .

- effective
- purposeful
- efficient
- thoughtful
- logical
- methodical
- correct
- responsive
- appropriate

APPEARANCE & PRESENTATION

The appearance and/or presentation of the students' work should . . .

- adhere to professional standards
- demonstrate craftsmanship
- align with "outside of school" role expectations
- use quality materials appropriately and effectively
- be fluent, smooth, elegant, polished
- be genuine/authentic

Reprinted with permission from *The High Performance Toolbox* (1998, Peak Learning Systems, Evergreen, Colorado).

2.50   RUBRIC DEVELOPMENT BY A SORTING TREE

PURPOSE

To facilitate the development of effective rubrics.

DESCRIPTION

The following is a simple procedure to facilitate the development of rubrics. The procedure is dependent on having numerous samples of student and/or professional work. This process is done with one characteristic at a time. The process is repeated for each important quality characteristic. (Limit the number of characteristics to 5 or fewer.)

USES

Quality

PROCEDURE

1. Determine what the rubric is for. (Examples: oral presentation, poster, problem solution, essay, etcetera)

2. Determine what the "impact" is that makes one high quality. (Examples: people learn from it, it persuades others, the solution is reasonable and usable, etcetera)

3. Determine the most important characteristic/attribute that makes it quality. (Examples: eye contact, thoroughness, logic, taste, appearance, organization, etcetera.)

4. Use the following sorting process for each characteristic/attribute identified in step 3.

   A. Sort the samples of student work into two piles for one of the characteristics/attributes identified in step 3 – okay and not okay.

   B. Take each of the two piles created above in step A and sort it into two piles based on quality.

   C. Continue this sorting only as long as is reasonable and important qualitative and/or quantitative distinctions can be made.

   Important Note: the number of levels (2,4,6, 8 or more) is determined by the context. Some characteristics will only have two discernible levels of quality – either it's quality or it's not. Also, two levels tend to be plenty for most daily efforts, four levels tend to be adequate for most products and performances, and more than four levels tends to be important for complex, continuously developing abilities like writing, speaking, skiing, and debating.

D. Verbalize the criteria that defines the targeted characteristic/attribute for each pile.

E. Maintain samples of student work to support and clarify each criteria.

Grade Level: *Elementary, Middle, High School*

Time: *Varies*

Special Materials: *None*

Motivational Standards: *Involving, Enabling, Successful*

Pluses: *Block Schedules, Group Processing, Multiple Intelligences*

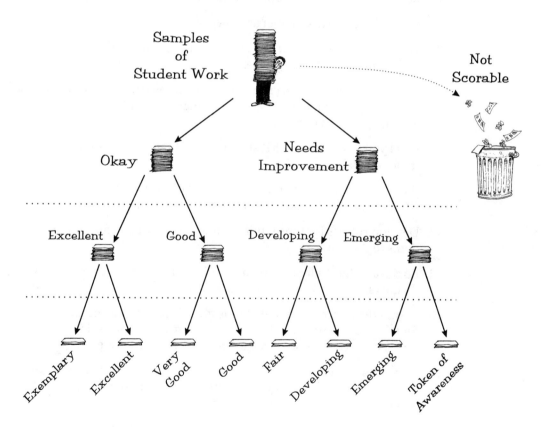

Reprinted with permission from *The High Performance Toolbox* (1998, Peak Learning Systems, Evergreen, Colorado).

QUICK TIP

2.51   RUBRICS - 17 QUICK TIPS

1. Involve students in the process of developing both the coaching and the scoring rubrics.

2. Develop rubrics that have an even number of identified quality levels.

3. Develop the second highest level first (very high quality).

4. Define a "B" really well, anything more than that is an "A," anything less isn't done yet. (Use this with a lot of small assignments and tasks that don't require a complex scoring scheme.)

5. Provide anchors (examples) that clarify what each portion of the rubric is describing.

6. Do not develop more levels for a scoring rubric than you can distinguish through important, qualitative descriptors.

7. Keep the language as simple as possible.

8. Keep all statements as brief and precise as possible.

9. Try not to provide a "laundry list" of characteristics for any given criteria or defined quality level.

10. Determine the essential criteria for a coaching or scoring rubric by identifying the quality characteristics that three diverse, exemplary examples have in common.

11. Limit your rubrics to addressing no more than seven criteria – but try for a maximum of three.

12. If you can't provide exemplary examples of student work for the students to use, do your best to create or find examples.

13. Develop rubrics for those "things" that are important for the students to do well.

14. Be certain the students have and understand the rubric before they do the task.

15. Do not develop more quality levels for a rubric than is reasonable for the task. Some tasks do not merit more than two levels – describe what good enough is and anything else isn't done yet.

16. Have students collect examples of rubrics from restaurants or other businesses. Use what they find to help develop understanding and support for being "rubric (quality) driven."

17. Establish criteria for how you will assign points for student work that falls between performance levels on the rubric.

2.52   SANDWICH CONSTRUCTIVE CRITICISM

If a student needs constructive criticism, build it into a sandwich. Start by pointing out specific good points about whatever has been done— even if the only thing is the amount of effort. Take the time to honor the student by identifying successes, effort, or value in the student work. Follow this with specific evidence of the difficulty, and conclude with more positive feedback. Also, provide the student with the opportunity to redo or improve what he/she has done.

Remember, the phrase "constructive criticism" is more comforting to the giver than the receiver.

2.53   SEEING THE WHOLE FOREST BEFORE THE TREES

Many learners become uncomfortable if they don't know where the lesson is going and how it's going to get there. Before starting a lesson or a unit, share both orally and in writing its intended outcomes and the strategies you have planned for getting there. Allow time for reflection and discussion. Some teachers like to ask for suggestions from the students at this point.

2.54   SELF-ASSESSMENT (REPORT) CARDS

PURPOSE

To provide a structure for regular student self-assessment of progress.

DESCRIPTION

When students are involved in the development of what is to be reported and shared with their parents, we see an increase in their level of commitment to their learning and progress.

In this strategy, develop mini self-assessment forms/cards for each area addressed by your school's report card. This works even better if you involve the students in developing the forms or cards with you.

USES

Motivational Environment, Quality

PROCEDURE

For each area being reported, put prompts on the form that are specific for the area, but appear something like this . . .

- What I've done best is . . . (provide example in portfolio.)
- The reasons I think so are . . .(be specific.)
- I'm having difficulty with . . . (provide evidence in portfolio.)
- I will improve the quality of my work by . . . (be specific.)
- The way in which my work is improving can be shown by . . . (provide evidence in portfolio.)

HINT

Refer to Chapter 6 for more self-assessment prompts.

Grade Level: *Elementary, Middle, High School*

Time: *On-going*

Special Materials: *5 x 7 cards*

Motivational Standards: *Successful, Involving*

Pluses: *Block Schedules*

2.55 SELF-PROGRESS CARDS

PURPOSE

To provide a vehicle by which students chart their progress in terms of information, skills, or concepts gained.

DESCRIPTION

Evidence of progress is very important to maintaining motivation. That's why so many dieters and athletes chart their progress in their efforts . . .

- pounds lost
- pounds pressed
- clothing sizes
- mileage run
- weekly weight
- times run

Though grades are an essential part of many schools' methods of reporting student progress, grades tend not to be effective for indicating progress for students. Scores on tests, quizzes, and projects just don't seem to accomplish the desired effect.

USES

Motivational Environment, Quality

PROCEDURE

1. Create a checklist, matrix, chart, or graph for the students that they can use to record what they have learned and what they have completed.

2. Teach the students how to use it, then devote time regularly for updating and reflection. To do this, it is necessary to determine what the students are improving or what they are gaining so they are able to indicate it as it occurs.

3. If a student has an alternative, but effective, way of charting his/her progress, accept it as an alternative. If the student is comfortable with you sharing the alternative method with the class, do so.

Grade Level: *Elementary, Middle, High School*

Time: *On-going*

Special Materials: *None*

Motivational Standards: *Successful, Involving*

Pluses: *Block Schedules*

2.56 S.E.T.A.
STUDENT EXPECTATIONS - TEACHER ACCOMPLISHMENT

PURPOSE

To increase student commitment and obtain essential guidance for maximum student achievement.

DESCRIPTION

SETA is a strategy in which the students are polled early in the school year to gain their input regarding what they feel they will need from you and your teaching in order to succeed at high levels. As mentioned in Chapter One, a critical key in achieving high levels of motivation is to involve the students in setting up standards. This strategy allows the students to be a part of setting the standards for the classroom. (This strategy combined with the strategy *Class Commitments* completes a powerful package for student involvement.)

USES

Motivational Environment, Quality

PROCEDURE

1. Start out by pledging your commitment to the success of everyone in the room. Tie your success to the students' success to begin creating a sense of community. At this point, some teachers ask the students why it is important that everyone, including you, be successful.

2. Ask the students to individually brainstorm on paper to determine everything they think that needs to be true about the class in order for everyone to be successful.

3. Have the students get into groups of 3-5 to share ideas and generate more – be certain to have the groups select facilitators, timekeepers, recorders, and reporters. Also at this stage, have the groups condense their ideas to the 3-5 that best convey *every* thought contributed. (Establish the shared condition that there is to be no judgment of any ideas and no discussion until all ideas are out.)

4. Take the ideas from each group and ask the class how they can be clumped and reduced to no more than seven statements that say it all.

5. Ask the students to go back to individual brainstorming to start the next phase. Have each student brainstorm the 3-7 expectations he/she needs to have met by the teacher if the results of steps 2-4 are to be achieved and have everyone successful.

6. Again, have the students form groups of 3-5 to share their teacher expectations, generate more, and condense.

7. Have each group share, and boil their responses down to no more than seven. Typical expectations may include . . .

   - be patient

   - explain clearly

   - allow enough time

   - don't embarrass us

   - help us whenever we need it

   - give us second chances if we mess up

   - make the class interesting and fun

8. Ask for student volunteers to create a nice poster listing the *Student Expectations for the Teacher* – post it prominently and commit to it.

   Note: Before receiving the student input, make it clear that you can not violate school policies or parent and community expectations. Also, move on to *Class Commitments* and involve students in establishing *Expectations for the Students*.

9. Visit the expectations regularly to assess progress.

Grade Level: Elementary, Middle, High School

Time: 30 minutes

Motivational Standards: Involving, Safe, Successful

Pluses: Block Schedules, Group Processing, Multiple Intelligences

A Special Thanks to Jim Ludington for this strategy.

2.57   STANDARDS OF EXCELLENCE

PURPOSE

To engage students in the development of coaching or scoring rubrics for a given project, product, or performance.

DESCRIPTION

This is a strategy proven to be effective as a means of helping students develop very high standards of excellence for a project, product, or performance.

USES

Motivational Environment, Quality

PROCEDURE

1. Determine specifically what the students are to be developing or doing.

2. Determine specifically what that project, product, or performance is intended to show as evidence of skill, ability, knowledge, and/or specifically what that project, product, or performance is supposed to be able to accomplish.

3. Obtain (or develop yourself) three models of exemplary projects, products, or performances based on the decisions in number two above. (These are called "exemplars.") The three models should have the similar characteristics that make them good models, but they should be diverse in how they do that. The models do not have to be perfect, but they do have to show what is identified in number two above.

4. Obtain (or develop yourself) at least one model that exemplifies what is absolutely <u>not</u> supposed to happen.

5. Divide the class into random groups of two to five depending on their group process skills.

6. Give the groups the three exemplars, clarify with them what they are and what they are intended to show and/or accomplish.

7. Ask the groups to begin comparing and contrasting the three exemplars in order to identify the three to five characteristics they have in common. Tell them you will interrupt the process shortly to provide them with NON-exemplary examples to help them focus their discussions.

8. Monitor the groups. When you judge that the non-exemplars would be helpful, pass them out to the groups.

9. While the groups are working, put 3 sheets of butcher paper on the wall, labeled as follows:

  - Characteristics that we all observe.

  - Characteristics that most of us observe.

  - Characteristics that at least one group observes.

10. Have the groups report, one at a time, the common characteristics. Poll the groups, and then have a recorder place the characteristics on the appropriate piece of butcher paper.

11. Have the groups discuss what's on the non-unanimous charts and decide if what's there should be moved to "characteristics that we all observe."

12. Facilitate a discussion with the groups to clarify the language on what all the groups now will agree are the three to five common characteristics. Be certain to probe for quality terms.

13. Use strategy number 2.50 "Rubric Development by a Sorting Tree" if scoring or developmental levels are desired..

Grade Level: Elementary, Middle, High School

Time: Varies

Special Materials: Examples of high quality student work, chart paper, markers, tape

Motivational Standards: Involving, Enabling

Pluses: Block Schedules, Group Processing

2.58 START WITH MOTIVATING QUESTIONS

Before beginning instruction, ask questions that are of interest to the students and that will be answered by the instruction. One example is, "How many of us are concerned about animals becoming extinct?"

2.59 STUDENTS RESPOND TO BEING LIKED - 4 QUICK TIPS

1. Provide sincere and appropriate compliments. Actively seek out opportunities to compliment students.

2. Devote several moments on a regular basis to informally "interview" students to learn about them. Show genuine interest.

3. Provide non-evaluative, immediate feedback openly. Avoid responding to students' contributions by varying responses with words like great, good, very nice, super, fantastic, and WOW. If this is happening rapid fire, the students will quickly place varying evaluative meaning to your responses that was unintended. Try "thank you" as a means of sincerely recognizing contributions.

4. Learn and use student names as quickly as possible, including correct spelling and pronounciation. Some ways to do this include:

    • if possible, have students make name cards for their desks

    • pass back papers personally and say each name as you hand it to the student

    • plan for and participate in "ice breaker" activities

    • use an alphabetized seating chart until each student is familiar to you

    • when necessary, write phonetic spellings on your seating chart and roster

    • learn what name or nickname a student prefers. for example: James or Jim or Jimmy.

2.60 TAKE-A-CHANCE CARDS

As teachers, we often wish that students would take a chance and try something new. Take-A-Chance Cards are to help students believe that it is indeed okay to try something creative.

> ## Take A Chance!
>
> I have a great idea and want to give it a try. I've checked it thoroughly. I sincerely believe it will accomplish what's expected by our assignment.
>
> Submitting this card with the completion of my idea protects me from any consequences if my idea doesn't work. I realize I will still be responsible for completing the assignment. For this card to be valid, I must keep my teacher informed of my progress throughout my effort.
>
> Peak Performers Take Reasonable Chances

Prepare Take-A-Chance cards like the one above. (Or, take a chance and design your own!) At the beginning of each grading period, give one card to each student. If, at any time, the student feels the desire to complete a task in some unusual way and it doesn't work out well, the student is to show you what they did and give you his/her Take-A-Chance Card. The card does not excuse the student from completing whatever was expected with the task. The card just excuses the student from any consequence for being late.

For a student to be entitled to use his/her card, you may want to ask that they inform you ahead of time that they are taking a chance. This would be a good opportunity to offer nurturing, non-stifling, guidance. This would also be the time that you could reach agreement as to when the task needs to be completed if the "idea" doesn't work out well.

Take A Chance!

I have a great idea and want to give it a try. I've checked it thoroughly. I sincerely believe it will accomplish what's expected by our assignment.

Submitting this card with the completion of my idea protects me from any consequences if my idea doesn't work. I realize I will still be responsible for completing the assignment. For this card to be valid, I must keep my teacher informed of my progress throughout my effort.

Peak Performers Take Reasonable Chances

Take A Chance!

I have a great idea and want to give it a try. I've checked it thoroughly. I sincerely believe it will accomplish what's expected by our assignment.

Submitting this card with the completion of my idea protects me from any consequences if my idea doesn't work. I realize I will still be responsible for completing the assignment. For this card to be valid, I must keep my teacher informed of my progress throughout my effort.

Peak Performers Take Reasonable Chances

Take A Chance!

I have a great idea and want to give it a try. I've checked it thoroughly. I sincerely believe it will accomplish what's expected by our assignment.

Submitting this card with the completion of my idea protects me from any consequences if my idea doesn't work. I realize I will still be responsible for completing the assignment. For this card to be valid, I must keep my teacher informed of my progress throughout my effort.

Peak Performers Take Reasonable Chances

Take A Chance!

I have a great idea and want to give it a try. I've checked it thoroughly. I sincerely believe it will accomplish what's expected by our assignment.

Submitting this card with the completion of my idea protects me from any consequences if my idea doesn't work. I realize I will still be responsible for completing the assignment. For this card to be valid, I must keep my teacher informed of my progress throughout my effort.

Peak Performers Take Reasonable Chances

Take A Chance!

I have a great idea and want to give it a try. I've checked it thoroughly. I sincerely believe it will accomplish what's expected by our assignment.

Submitting this card with the completion of my idea protects me from any consequences if my idea doesn't work. I realize I will still be responsible for completing the assignment. For this card to be valid, I must keep my teacher informed of my progress throughout my effort.

Peak Performers Take Reasonable Chances

Take A Chance!

I have a great idea and want to give it a try. I've checked it thoroughly. I sincerely believe it will accomplish what's expected by our assignment.

Submitting this card with the completion of my idea protects me from any consequences if my idea doesn't work. I realize I will still be responsible for completing the assignment. For this card to be valid, I must keep my teacher informed of my progress throughout my effort.

Peak Performers Take Reasonable Chances

2.61   THE 6 ULTRA SUPREME LAWS
FOR HAVING A MOTIVATING CLASSROOM

1. Ensure that no student will be embarrassed or hurt.
2. Ensure that the learning will be interesting or valuable to the students, or embed it in what's interesting or valuable to them.
3. Ensure meaningful involvement of all students in setting direction and standards.
4. Ensure adequate evidence of progress and mastery.
5. Ensure each student feels included, cared for, and valued.
6. Ensure effective instructional practices for each student's needs.

QUICK TIP

2.62   THE 21 ESSENTIALS FOR
PRESERVING MOTIVATION

SAFE

1. Do not create situations in which students will feel stupid or incapable.
2. Do not create situations in which students may feel embarrassed.
3. Ensure that students are safe from physical harm.

QUICK TIP

VALUABLE

4. Ensure that what the students are to learn is something they value, need, want, or solves a problem they have.
5. Design instruction that addresses the essential content and the students' interests.
6. Ensure that the learning is challenging and possible for each student.
7. Ensure that the learning situation is fun or interesting for the student.

SUCCESSFUL

8. Provide regular evidence of progress or mastery.
9. Provide specific and timely feedback.

INVOLVING

10. Involve students meaningfully in establishing performance standards.
11. Provide meaningful opportunities for choices and decisions.
12. Provide numerous meaningful opportunities for each student to be involved or to respond (at least once every 10 minutes.)

CARING

13. Ensure that students' basic physical and emotional needs are met.

14. Listen sincerely.

15. Ensure feelings of inclusion.

16. Do not praise falsely or hollowly.

17. Praise and recognize each student in ways that meet his/her individual needs.

18. Strive to relate with students.

ENABLING

19. Use instructional strategies and techniques that are effective for each student.

20. Model what you teach.

21. Provide examples.

QUICK TIP

2.63   USE "WHY?" CAUTIOUSLY

Why? Quite often when someone does something that others think shouldn't have been done, the question that is invariably asked is, "Why did you do that?" Examples we can all remember include the following:

"Why did you forget your books?"

"Why didn't you get the trash out in time?"

"Why did you eat so much right before dinner?"

"Why did you break it?"

"Why didn't you feed your younger brother like I asked you to?"

When many of us hear a question starting with "why" it puts us on edge. Try phrasing your questions differently to avoid the problem.

"What might have been the reasons that …?"

"How could it be that …?"

"What could have caused that …?"

In *The Tale of Two Cities*, why did …? (Notice that the word *why* is not at the beginning of the question.)

2.64 VANITY PLATES

PURPOSE

To introduce students to each other.

DESCRIPTION

A fun, easy, and quick way to have students introduce themselves to each other is through the use of personalized license plates or "Vanity Plates." The real Vanity Plates are designed to reveal something about the owner in a quick, yet clever way. The classroom Vanity Plates are exactly the same!

USES

Motivational Environment

PROCEDURE

1. Share numerous examples of real-world Vanity Plates with the students. Have the students compile a list of similar traits they see in all or most of the examples that make them "exemplars" (examples of exemplary work).

2. Have the students create personal Vanity Plates that will denote something unique or interesting about themselves and adhere to the quality criteria previously identified.

3. Have the students share their Vanity Plates and then post them around the room.

4. Have the students write a short essay explaining and justifying why they did their Vanity Plates the way they did.

5. If the students actually need more time when the time is up, repeat the process with a slight variation. First, give the groups that need more time 20 seconds to decide how much time they need. Then poll the groups and give them the amount of time you think they need and is within the time limits given by the students.

6. Before you ask them to begin again, tell the students what they should do if their group finishes before the time is up.

7. When the time is up, be certain you have a meaningful, value added discussion planned that will allow a group that needs more time to finish quickly.

Grade Level: Elementary, Middle, High School

Time: 20 minutes

Special Materials: Construction paper or 5 x 7 index cards, markers, tape

Motivational Standards: Involving, Caring

Pluses: Block Schedules, Group Processing, Multiple Intelligences

QUICK TIP

2.65 "WAIT-TIME" MANAGEMENT

Wait time is difficult for a lot of us. One idea that helps us get through the time and validates those students who always have an answer right away is the *quick nod*. Let the students know that from this point forward you will nod to validate students as they raise their hands, but you won't call on anyone until sufficient wait time has occurred.

QUICK TIP

2.66 WE'RE IN THIS TOGETHER

When things are tough, students like to know they're not alone. Take time out to add a truthful and comforting comment like . . .

- "A lot of people feel as you do. How many others agree with Bill?"

- "I can tell you're worried about the assignment. Most of us are concerned too."

- "It's normal to feel nervous about giving a speech in front of the class. How many of us are feeling nervous?"

- "A lot of people feel as you do, but I have a different opinion. "

- "What we're doing is difficult at first. I had a lot of trouble the first time I did it too."

- "Help me understand what you're feeling. Can you tell me more?"

- "Thank you for being honest about not being ready. I'll get back to you when you're ready."

- "Thanks for volunteering. I appreciate the risk you took."

2.67 WHEN WILL I EVER USE THIS STUFF?

PURPOSE

To help students understand the importance of what they are learning.

DESCRIPTION

Quite often, particularly in the higher grade levels, students begin to question why they should have to learn what is being taught. Though we cannot guarantee that every student will use everything that they are learning, we do know that people tend to learn better if they see a potential use for what they are learning.

This activity uses the concept of an art gallery in which the students display photographs, drawings, tapes, or other artifacts from outside of school that quickly show how what they are learning is important or used by people in their community. The activity is done at the beginning of a unit and, therefore, should not require the students to go into great depth.

USES

Motivational Environment

PROCEDURE

1. Identify the significant concepts or skills the students will be learning.

2. Depending on the nature of what is to be learned, have the students obtain photographs, make drawings, gather clippings, make or collect tapes that provide evidence that the learning is used or applied in a way that impacts their lives. (Examples are triangles in bridge and home construction, optics in glasses, misconceptions in letters to the editor, or references to literature in articles.)

3. Have the students display their evidence in the classroom, a display case, or before younger students.

Grade Level: Elementary, Middle, High School

Time: Variable

Special Materials: None

Motivational Standards: Valuable, Involving, Enabling

Pluses: Block Schedules, Group Processing, Multiple Intelligences

CHAPTER 3

MAKING TEACHING EASIER

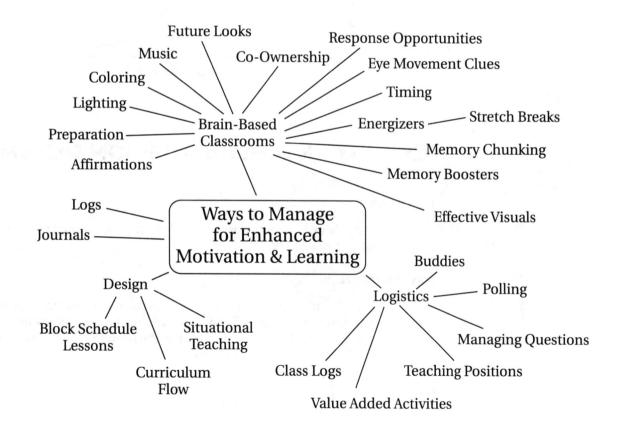

QUICK TIP

3.1　BALANCING STRESSES

Recent brain research indicates that as a student's level of stress is increased there is an increase in learning. However, if the stress is raised beyond a certain point, the brain "down shifts" and the quality of learning actually decreases. (Recent research shows that "down shifting" is not an accurate metaphor, but it still helps people to realize the importance of meeting students' emotional needs.) Each student responds differently to different conditions that increase both positive and negative stress. **Therefore, it is crucial to monitor each student carefully and make adjustments to maintain the maximum quality levels of learning and performance.** It may prove beneficial to survey the students to determine what in classrooms typically raises desire to perform well (positive stress) and what causes enough discomfort that the effect on learning is detrimental.

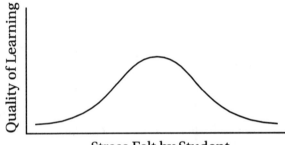

3.2　BLOCK SCHEDULE LESSON DESIGN

PURPOSE

To provide one of many possible models for lesson design that can be used with block schedules.

DESCRIPTION

Block schedules offer the luxury of adequate time for using strategies and techniques that are effective for building deeper understanding. The other side of this issue, however, is the need to provide enough transitions to keep things interesting and active.

USES

Lesson Design

PROCEDURE

This model tends to be most comfortable for teachers coming from a traditional background. It involves designing units or lessons based on three deliberate phases.

1. *Acquisition* of information/skills/concepts (approximately one-third to one-half of the available time).

2. *Application* of information/skills/concepts (approximately one-half to one-third of the available time).

3. *Closure* through connections, reflections, and projections (approximately one-sixth of the available time).

Teachers who plan their block schedule lessons in three phases such as these tend to be successful. (Dr. Robert Lynn Canady and Michael D Rettig, *Block Scheduling: A Catalyst for Change in High Schools* (1995), Eye on Education, Princeton, NJ)

During the *acquisition phase*, use the best available instructional practices to teach the desired information, skills, or concepts. Then provide a transition to move into phase two.

The *application phase* is the time during which the students are engaged in activities which require them to use or apply what they acquired in phase one. This is the phase in which the students begin to gain understanding – if it is cut short, the learning and retention will suffer. This phase should require the students to go beyond mere practicing or recall of the content that has been presented. Before moving to the closure phase, provide a transition.

The *closure phase* is crucial, for it is during this time that the students' minds are actively engaged in forming connections, reflecting, self-assessing, reviewing, projecting to other uses or steps. This is when the students are actively *lingering over their learning*.

During transitions, be sure to get the students moving and to engage them in activities that will help form mental bridges for them.

Grade Level: *Elementary, Middle, High School*

Time: *On-going*

Motivational Standards: *Enabling*

Pluses: *Block Schedules*

3.3   CARBON COPIES

Keep plenty of carbon paper on hand. The office supply stores will love you for taking it off their hands, and it will help you monitor student work. Whenever you ask the students to make entries into their journals, logs, or notebooks, and would like an easy way of collecting their entries, have them make carbon copies.

3.4   CHALK THAT PEOPLE CAN SEE: "SIDEWALK CHALK"

Most of us no longer depend on chalk boards. There are many reasons for this, but one reason is that it is very difficult for many students to see what is written on the board from the seats toward the back of the room.

At last there is a solution. It was developed many years ago by railroaders. It was called railroad chalk until it became available in toy stores for kids as "sidewalk chalk." This chalk is much thicker, and therefore much brighter than the chalk we typically see in school. Most large office, variety, and engineering supply stores carry it.

3.5   CLASS LOGS

PURPOSE

To provide a daily student generated record of class objectives, activities, and assignments.

DESCRIPTION

WHEN STUDENTS HAVE MISSED CLASS, THEY CHECK THE CLASS LOG TO SEE WHAT HAPPENED DURING THEIR ABSENCES

A Class Log is a loose-leaf notebook containing student generated records describing what happened during each class period. When students have missed class, they check the class log to see what happened during their absences. It is also a great aid for students who have trouble with important concepts even though they are present during the lesson.

Class Logs typically include the following:

- statements clarifying major lesson topics and objectives,

- specific examples used as part of the instruction,

- instructional activities that were used throughout the lesson,

- important questions that were asked during class and the responses given,

- important announcements that were made pertaining to the class or school in general,

- assignments and due dates, and

- copies of handouts given during class.

USES

Classroom Management

PROCEDURE

1. Develop the Class Log entries yourself for the first week of school so students will have quality models to follow when they assume responsibility for the task.

2. After the first few days, distribute copies of the teacher generated Class Log entries. Allot time for reviewing and discussing them. It is very important that students understand the purpose for the Class Log and the significance of each section.

3. Teach the students that the job of the Class Log recorders involves:

   - taking very accurate and complete notes about what happens in class,

   - using their notes and other support materials to create the Class Log entries, and

   - adding their entries to the Class Log.

4. Ensure that students know that if they are absent on a day they are responsible for the Class Log, it is their responsibility to arrange for a substitute. One of the side benefits of this strategy is that it provides a context for responsible behavior. If a student fails to arrange for a substitute, arrange for a volunteer to swap days with the absent student.

5. Periodically evaluate the students' entries. Their entries can count as a homework assignment and be graded accordingly.

6. Once the rotation through the class has been completed, create a new schedule and resume the process.

HINT

Create a pre-printed Class Log page that each student uses when it is his/her turn. Print large quantities and place them in a central location for easy student access.

Grade Level: Middle, High School

Time: On-going

Special Materials: 3-ring loose leaf binder, pre-printed "Class Log" pages

Motivational Standards: Enabling, Involving

Pluses: Block Schedules

Class Log

Name

Date

Page ___ of ___

Complete your class log by explaining what happened in class. Use the following order for your log. Attach copies of any handouts.

- Objectives
- Important points
- Activities
- Questions asked by the teacher & answers
- Questions & answers from students
- Assignments & due dates
- Handouts
- Announcements
- Other

QUICK TIP

3.6 CLASSROOMS CONDUCIVE TO LEARNING

The following checklist is to provide guidance in ensuring your classroom is conducive to learning:

____ 1. The walls are painted in pastels of green, blue, or aqua tones. Light yellows are also okay. Paneling, brick, and cork can add a pleasant warmth.

____ 2. There are water containers, plants, or humidifiers to prevent the air from becoming too dry.

____ 3. Instructional materials are on the side walls with …

    ____ A. concept posters, content reminders, and review materials that you want the students to be able to recall placed above eye level. This will put the students in a visual mode.

    ____ B. announcements, assignments, and special messages placed at eye level. This will put the students in an auditory mode.

    ____ C. student work and evidence of progress (not grades) placed below eye level. This will put the students in a kinesthetic mode and tap positive feelings.

    ____ D. affirmations, positive posters, and other inspirational displays placed high. This will put the students in a visual mode.

____ 4. Lighting is as "full spectrum" as possible. Avoid florescent lights if at all possible. Enhance lighting with incandescent lamps.

____ 5. There are no obstacles or objects between yourself and the students.

____ 6. The room arrangement permits you being as close as possible to each student.

____ 7. The room is arranged to create feelings of spaciousness.

____ 8. The room temperature is comfortable – between 68 and 72 degrees Fahrenheit.

____ 9. There is plenty of ventilation and fresh air.

Adapted from *Super Teaching* (1995, Turning Point Publishing). Thanks to the author Eric Jenson of Del Mar, California.

3.7   CONCEPTS ON THE WALL

Before starting a lesson or a unit, design and display a large poster or flip chart with a word or short phrase and a clarifying sketch for each of the major concepts you will be teaching. Be sure the poster or flip-chart is easy to see and very visible. Refer to your poster as you first begin instruction regarding each concept.

QUICK TIP

3.8   DAILY CLASSROOM PREPARATION

In order to help students be prepared to learn, prepare your classroom for each lesson. The following checklist can help:

QUICK TIP

____ 1. The room is neat and well organized.

____ 2. Chairs and tables are arranged as needed.

____ 3. Books, handouts, and needed materials are counted and ready.

____ 4. Room temperature is between 68 and 72 degrees Fahrenheit.

____ 5. Chalk boards and chart paper are free of unneeded information. Only greetings and needed directions are displayed.

____ 6. There is adequate ventilation and fresh air.

3.9   DIRECT TEACHING

PURPOSE

To provide a model for direct instruction of students.

DESCRIPTION

This is a seven step approach for providing direct instruction from introduction to application of knowledge.

PROCEDURE

1. The "What" – What the students are to learn is made clear to the students through clear language and meaningful examples.

2. The "Why" – The students are provided with the rationale for learning what they are to learn. This is provided in student language or through discussion or discovery.

3. The "How" – The students are taught through modeling, "think aloud," "concept attainment," and other effective strategies.

4. Guided Practice – The students are provided ample opportunities to practice and experiment with what is being taught in group situations, with feedback from peers and the teacher.

5. Independent Practice – The students are provided with ample opportunities to practice on their own and then to engage in debriefing and feedback sessions with peers.

6. Self-Direction – The teacher gradually pulls back using an "I–We–They" approach to develop competence and confidence in the students.

7. Application – The students are given opportunities to use and refine their skills in new and rich contexts.

Grade Levels: *Elementary, Middle, High School*

Time: *On-going*

Special Materials: *None*

Motivational Standards: *Enabling*

Pluses: *Block Schedules*

Adapted from a workshop conducted by Bobb Darnell of District 214, Arlington Heights, Illinois.

3.10 DOOR GREETINGS

QUICK TIP

Greet the students at the door. Use their names—no one can ignore the sound of his or her own name. Also, before beginning an instruction, try to scan the room and make eye contact with each student. Winks, nods, and other welcoming gestures are great also, but be certain to be completely equitable.

3.11   DRIP, SPLASH, AND FLOOD

Don't try to teach everything there is about any given topic all at once. Spread learning over time and students will learn it better, with less pain, and remember it longer.

QUICK TIP

To understand this concept, picture the effects of water when there are long lasting drips, quick splashes, and deep floods. Steady drips over time will erode holes through solid concrete and rocks. A quick splash gets everything wet for a moment, then everything dries and is as it was. A flood soaks deep into the ground.

First introduce a topic with a quick splash. Throw out the ideas, toss them around, play with them, and go on to something else. Don't test during the splash phase - it's just to lay the groundwork.

Use a flood to teach the concept that was splashed a few times during previous units. During this phase, provide in-depth skill and concept development strategies.

Use the drip method to keep bringing back what was flooded earlier. Long term learning will develop because of these drips (distributed practice.)

Thanks to Iris Mcginnis for introducing us to this metaphor.

3.12   EYE MOVEMENT CLUES FOR DETERMINING THINKING STYLES

BACKGROUND EXPLANATION

QUICK TIP

With many people, the movement of their eyes provide clues as to their thinking styles. Watch your students' eyes during phases of your lessons in order to gain insights as to how to better meet their needs. For example, use eye movements to determine which students are likely visual learners and which are primarily auditory learners.

There are seven eye positions that can indicate thinking style. Use them as clues, but be careful not to depend on them too much. Also, for many left handed students, the eye movements will be opposite of what they are for right handed students.

The graphic included with this tip will help to clarify the following patterns:

1.   Creating Images – When students' eyes move to the upper right, they are probably creating pictures or images. You can check for this

pattern with people by asking them questions that will cause them to create images such as: "What would you look like with gray hair and a beard?" "What would you look like if you were a foot taller?" "How would an elephant look with a buffalo's coat?"

2. Recalling Images – Students are probably recalling images or pictures when their eyes move to the upper left. You can check for this by asking questions such as: "What did your mom look like when you last saw her this morning?" "What does your kitchen look like?" "What did you look like five years ago?"

3. Creating Sound – When students' eyes move horizontally to the right, they are probably determining what something might sound like. You can check for this by asking questions such as: "What would a dog sound like if it could talk?" "Create a tune in your head – what does it sound like?" "What would it sound like if you were listening to jazz, classical, rock music all at once?"

4. Recalling Sound – Students are probably recalling sounds when their eyes move horizontally and to the left. You can check for this by asking questions such as: "What's the fifth word in our national anthem?" "What does your favorite piece of music sound like?" "What did the last person say to you as you left home this morning?"

5. Experiencing Feelings – When students' eyes move downward and to the right, they are probably experiencing feelings. You can check for this by asking questions that will foster an immediate emotional response. When this happens, in many cases the eyes will drop rapidly, then rise back to the center to continue an answer. To generate questions to check for this eye movement, it is very helpful to have some knowledge of what might trigger an emotional response. The following is an example question that might work. "Have you finished cleaning your room (like you promised)?"

6. Conversing with Self – When people are carrying on conversations with themselves, quite often their eyes will drop to the lower left. You might best test this by carrying on a conversation with yourself while checking where your eyes are comfortable at the time.

7. Recalling Memorized Information – Students' eyes will tend to stay dead center when they are recalling or using information that is solidly memorized. Check this by asking questions that require no thought such as: "What is your name?" "What's your address and phone number?" Questions like "How are you today?" will tend to produce the same eye movement because most of us answer with well memorized and practiced responses.

COMMON EYE MOVEMENTS

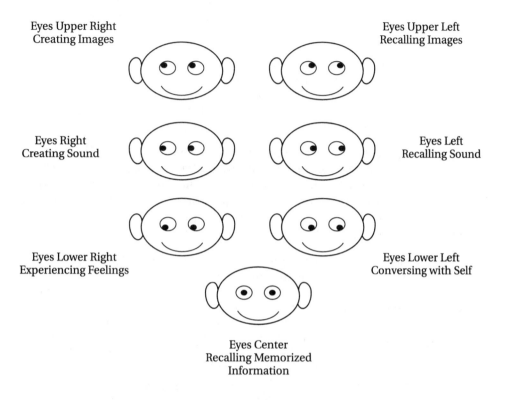

Eyes Upper Right
Creating Images

Eyes Upper Left
Recalling Images

Eyes Right
Creating Sound

Eyes Left
Recalling Sound

Eyes Lower Right
Experiencing Feelings

Eyes Lower Left
Conversing with Self

Eyes Center
Recalling Memorized
Information

5 QUICK TIPS FOR USING EYE MOVEMENTS TO IMPROVE STUDENT LEARNING

1. Help students discover their most appropriate and comfortable eye positions. Encourage them to use those positions at appropriate times, when trying to remember what was on the board several days before.

2. Stand on the right side of your classroom (from your students' perspective) when presenting new information.

3. When reviewing, make sure you are on your students' left side.

4. During tests, spread the students' desks out enough so you can comfortably encourage the students to let their eyes wander to help recall or build responses.

5. Put students' work on the wall …

   • above eye level if you want the students to be able to recall it easily;

   • at eye level if you are going to have discussions about it; and

   • below eye level if you want to encourage feelings about it.

Adapted from *Super Teaching* (1995, Turning Point Publishing). Thanks to the author Eric Jenson of Del Mar, California.

QUICK TIP

3.13 ENERGIZERS KEEP STUDENTS' BRAINS ACTIVE - 9 QUICK TIPS

Many of us are uncomfortable doing energizers with our students in high school or above. However, energizers are important to learners of all ages. How your students react to them will be greatly influenced by how you feel about them. If you value them, your students will most likely value them also.

What follows are several energizers that can be easily adapted to fit your circumstances. We like to get more than one benefit from each activity by adapting it to be an energizer that addresses content also, but feel free to use them however they work best for you.

1. SUPPORT IMITATORS

Ask the students to get in pairs, think up a machine like a car, boat, or computer, and then role play how it works.

2. HAND-TOSS REVIEW

Have the students get in a circle and toss a ball from one to the other. Whoever catches the ball is to say something they remember learning or a connection they have made. If students have trouble catching, you can have them number off (up to six) and roll a die.

3. STRETCHES

Ask the students to stand beside their seats and reach as high as they can. Have them shake their hands in the air. Then have them stand up and down on their tip-toes.

4. RUN ON'S

Ask the students to form circles of five to seven students each. Identify a starter for each group. Have all the starters begin a sentence about what they have been studying and stop early into the sentence. The person next to them is to add to the sentence meaningfully, and so on. If a sentence gets completed, the next person is to start a new one. Encourage the students to keep the sentence going as long as possible.

5. SONGS

Lead the class in singing a song they all enjoy and is meaningful to them. Allow people to join in as they choose.

6. REPORTERS

Have the students form pairs. One person in the pair is to be the reporter for a major television news show – have them actually pick names of famous reporters. The other person is to play the role of a content expert being interviewed for the evening news. Give each team two to three minutes to conduct their interviews.

7. COMMERCIALS

Have the students form groups of four or five. Give the groups ten minutes to develop a commercial that reviews important points from what they've been studying. Ask them to limit their commercials in time (30 seconds) but not in creativity and fun. Give the students time to present their commercials to the class.

8. SWITCH SEATS

Ask everyone to stand and move to a new seat in the classroom.

9. TOPIC PLAY-OFFS

Have the students form groups of three to five. Give them a list of the topics you have been teaching. Assign one topic to each person in the groups. Give them several minutes to each try to convince the others that their topics are the most important. Then ask them as a group to pick the one topic that has the most evidence supporting it as the most important topic. Have the groups prepare a 45 second presentation supporting their selected most important topic – their presentation is to contain at least three strong arguments.

3.14   FAIR AND VALUING SEATING

Provide equal value seating. Arrange seats in a circle so that all positions convey equal value. If the circular arrangement requires two rings, alternate who's in the first or second ring by "even day - odd day."

3.15   FAST TIMING

Keep your lessons moving quickly, taking extreme care to eliminate any time that any students are sitting idle. Before beginning a lesson, be certain everything you need is ready, so you can keep things flowing. The students will learn to expect things to move quickly.

If down time is expected for some students, be certain there is something for them to do. If nothing else, provide inexpensive toys or blocks for the students to play with. The kinesthetic learners will love you for it. Surprisingly, this is true even for high school students and adult learners.

3.16   FRAME YOUR OVERHEAD TRANSPARENCIES

If you don't want to purchase a special frame, use cardboard to make a frame that your transparencies can drop into while you're projecting them. This will block unnecessary glare, while visually framing your message.

3.17   HELP STUDENTS BE CO-OWNERS OF THE CLASSROOM

Rather than filling the walls of the classroom with posters (a few with positive affirmations are always nice) have students create posters, mind maps, pictures, and other valued artifacts to put on the walls. As humans, we have basic territory needs. Help this by involving the students in co-developing the classroom. This way it is easier to develop a joint pride and sense of ownership that can result in greater motivation to keep the classroom picked-up and nice. Try a "getting to know you" area in which each student posts either a drawing, favorite song, photograph, or quote. Try a recent project wall on which the students display artifacts from a recent project or activity.

Adapted from workshops by Doug McPhee and his book, *Limitless Learning: Making Powerful Learning an Everyday Event* (1996, Zephyr Press).

3.18 HOMEWORK BUDDIES

PURPOSE

To facilitate the identification and/or review of important concepts.

DESCRIPTION

Assigning "homework buddies" can be a very effective way to review homework. Most students enjoy helping and working with each other. Also, when students explain the homework, concepts, questions or problems to each other, their comprehension of the concepts increases.

USES

Classroom Management

PROCEDURE

1. Assign or have students choose a partner with whom they will work and study for a given period of time. This may vary from 1 week to 1 month.

2. Give students a block of time to help each other with the homework.

3. Facilitate the homework discussions, then have a whole class discussion of homework questions or problems that seem to be difficult for many students.

HINT

Take the time before starting this strategy to have students identify and practice good team behaviors.

> *Grade Level:* Elementary, Middle, High School
>
> *Time:* 10-30 minutes
>
> *Special Materials:* None
>
> *Motivational Standards:* Enabling
>
> *Pluses:* Block Schedules, Group Processing

3.19 JOURNALS, DAILY OR WEEKLY

PURPOSE

To provide for self-reflection and assessment, and to facilitate improved communication between students and teachers.

DESCRIPTION

With this strategy, the students are asked to keep a journal. The journal is used much like a diary in that the students use it regularly to record their thoughts, feelings, recollections, or insights into their learning.

Based on budget considerations, there are numerous options for the students to use as journals:

- small writing tablets,

- sets of 25-50 sheets of regular school paper that have been stapled along the left margin,

- sets of five to ten sheets of regular school paper, folded in half, and stabled along the fold to make miniature writing booklets, or

- folders with packs of 10-20 sheets of paper that have been stapled together.

USES

Instruction, Reflection

PROCEDURE

Journal

Linger Over Learning

1. Either ask the students to purchase what they will use for journals or provide what they are to use. Provide a journal cover like the one shown here or have students create their own cover page.

2. Before beginning the use of journals, facilitate a discussion with the students as to the potential benefits of journals. This is also the appropriate time to work with the students to develop guidelines for journal entries and feedback. The following are recommended:

   - Quality journal entries are an expectation – journals are a means of communicating much like a telephone.

   - Entries will not be graded. Journal entries will not effect grades, however normal courtesies are urged for maintaining positive relationships.

   - The quality of the entries is based more on content than grammar or spelling.

- Thoughts recorded in a journal are just that. They will not be evaluated as right or wrong.

- Journal entries are confidential; be honest.

- If you cannot respond to a prompt, try to explain why not.

- Writing is to be in a conversational tone as if it is a piece of writing to a friend.

- Your journal is yours, but it is our way of conversing. To protect your journal, I will record my thoughts to you on self-sticking notes.

3. Periodically, whenever reflection would be beneficial to the students' progress or to your assessment of progress, ask the students to record their reflections in their journals. Reflections can be completely open or responses to prompts like the following:

    - Of all that we've done today, what's been most helpful to you?

    - How might you use what we've learned this week?

    - During our lesson today, what was most confusing to you?

    - What questions do you have about what we're learning?

    - If you were the teacher, what might you have done differently to have made learning easier?

    Refer to Chapter six for numerous additional ideas for prompts.

4. Pick up five or six journals at random each day you have the students make entries. Read them, respond immediately, and get them back.

5. Periodically, you can pick up all the journals for your review, but get them back by the next day.

Grade Level: Elementary, Middle, High School

Time: Ongoing

Special Materials: Journals for the students

Motivational Standards: Enabling, Involving

Pluses: Block Schedules

Journal

Linger Over Learning

3.20 KEEP 'EM GUESSING

Routine is comfortable, but routine can provide too much comfort. Keep enough variety in how you do things so that there is a *safe* level of unpredictability.

QUICK TIP

3.21 KEEP MOVING

Most of us have heard the phrase, "It's easier to see a moving target." The reason is simple. As humans, we naturally spot movement. Use this fact to keep interest up in the classroom. Keep moving – however, be careful to go to your power position before beginning a session.

QUICK TIP

3.22 KNOW THE CLASSROOM

Take time before starting the year or whenever you re-arrange your room to know your classroom. Walk around the room and check everything carefully. Stand and sit every place a student will and make sure it is conducive to learning. Check for visibility, hearing, and temperature. The better you know the classroom, the more at home you'll feel and the better you'll meet the needs of your students.

QUICK TIP

3.23 LOST TEACHING IDEAS

Tried a good idea lately? If so, write it in your next year's calendar so you won't forget it.

Ever wonder why we forget so many good teaching ideas from year to year? Beverly Joyce Showers has shared an interesting discovery regarding this problem from her research. In general, people, have to do something twenty-eight times for it to become part of their natural behavior.

QUICK TIP

QUICK TIP

3.24 MEMORY BOOSTERS
13 QUICK TIPS FOR IMPROVING MEMORY IN THE CLASSROOM

There are many things we can do as teachers to increase how much students remember. The Memory Boosters are all powerful tools – we invite you to pick one to practice each week to help the students remember important content.

Make it personal

1. Connect what you want them to remember to a strong emotion through a moving story, song, or activity.

2. Personalize it by using the students' names and things they can relate to from their homes and neighborhoods.

3. Act it out as a skit or role play in a way the students think is fun.

4. Present and review it in all of our senses: sight, sound, touch, taste, and smell.

5. Embed it in a real-life application the students relate to and value.

6. Make it important to know.

Use good memory tools

7. Use distributed exposure – repeat it within 10 minutes, then again in 30 minutes, repeat it the next day, then in two days, then five, and so on.

8. Help the students develop concrete connections and reminders.

9. Have the students summarize it in words or mind maps.

10. Have the students draw a picture that represents it.

11. Use acronyms.

12. Use *Memory Chunking* – no more than seven things to remember in any category.

13. Put it on a colorful, easily-seen poster, and display it above eye height on the students' left. (See "Eye Movement Clues for Determining Thinking Styles" for more information about positioning and eye movement.)

3.25 MEMORY CHUNKING

Recent brain research indicates that there are reasonable limits to what people can store in their short term memories. Within a topic, **keep the number of points (chunks) the students are to remember limited** to the number indicated by the following chart. The "plus or minus 2" in the chart indicates that some students in the age range may be able to remember up to two more items, but others may be limited to two fewer items. (Thanks to Dr. Pat Wolfe for providing us with this information – based on the work of Juan Pascual-Leon, 1970.)

Students' Ages	Number of Chunks
15 and older	7 plus or minus 2
13	6 plus or minus 2
11	5 plus or minus 2
9	4 plus or minus 2
7	3 plus or minus 2
5	2 plus or minus 2
3	1 plus or minus 2

When there is too much for the students to store in short term memory, look for ways to create chunks.

Example: grouping 15 formulas into five groups of three formulas each.

QUICK TIP

3.26 MUSIC HELPS PEOPLE LEARN

Use music in your classroom to help establish an appropriate atmosphere for the learning and activity, but take care to match the music to the desired effect.

For many of us, this is a difficult concept to try. We invite you to try it and see if it works for you. It will make a difference for kids.

When getting started, a tape player is the least expensive, but a CD system will give you more flexibility. If it fits in the budget, a remote control is wonderful in the classroom. Detachable speakers are also a great asset.

When using music, be gentle on your students' ears. Adjust volume levels slowly, and never go over what you have found to be a comfortable level for all of your students. Also, be certain to explain to your students why you are using music in the classroom, particularly if they are older students and are not used to teachers using it.

Use Baroque music for quiet activity, review, and anytime you want to establish a calm and peaceful atmosphere. Pieces to try include *Four Seasons* by Vivaldi or *Brandenburg Concertos* by Bach. There are also many wonderful selections available by Mozart, Pachelbel, and others. Be careful to get music by a full orchestra.

Try classical selections from Beethoven, Tchaikovsky, and Chopin for periods of active participation or engaging lectures.

Explore the use of New Age and nature music for relaxing times.

Experiment with music of today for those times when students are to be actively engaged in working on a project or task. Be certain to check for appropriateness of any lyrics before using a piece in your classroom.

Adapted from *Limitless Learning: Making Powerful Learning an Everyday Event* (1996, Zephyr Press) by Doug McPhee and *Super Teaching* (1995, Turning Point Publishing) by Eric Jenson. We strongly recommend adding both these resources to your library.

3.27 NOTES THAT STICK

Many students enjoy recording notes next to important points in books or handouts. Often it is not appropriate to write in the book, or the students just don't want to write in their books or directly on their handouts. Either provide "self-stick removable notes" for these students, or encourage them to supply their own.

3.28 OPEN WITH PERSONAL CONNECTIONS

QUICK TIP

Before beginning class, make eye contact with everyone. Nods, greetings, and kind words also help, but be certain to be equitable.

3.29 POLLING

PURPOSE

To gather essential information and student perspectives in a way that provides response opportunities without slowing down the class or opening the door to distractions.

USES

Classroom Management, Motivational Environment

PROCEDURE

Rather than asking questions like, "do any of you need more time?" ask, "how many need more time?" You can get more information faster without prompting conversation and side issues. Example polling questions include . . .

- "How many agree with what Ted is saying?"

- "How many think five more minutes will be enough?"

- "How many think it's okay that we work another five minutes and then check to see if more time is needed?"

- "How many are ready for the next set of directions?"

- "How many agree that's a problem?"

- "On three, hold up your hand if you think Columbus was the most courageous, or hold up a fist if you think Neil Armstrong was the most courageous."

- "Have one person in your group hold up from one to five fingers indicating how much time your group needs."

Grade Level: Elementary, Middle, High School

Time: 1 minute

Motivational Standards: Involving

3.30 PROVIDE A LOOK INTO THE FUTURE

With new materials such as books and manuals, provide time for the students to become familiar with them before they are expected to use them. Devote class time to the students looking through the materials, jotting down observations, noting things of interest, or generating questions. You can even ask each student to find one thing in the book to describe, explain, or tell someone else about. Provide time for each student or group to report their findings, and respond to any questions that surface.

Adapted from a workshop conducted by Doug McPhee at the National Staff Development Council Conference in Vancouver, British Columbia.

3.31 QUESTION BOXES

PURPOSE

To provide a forum for student questions.

DESCRIPTION

Many students are uncomfortable asking some questions in front of their classmates yet their learning would be enhanced if they had a way to get their questions answered. Also, many times students will have questions they would like to have answered, but they do not ask them because they know the questions are off topic enough to distract the class. This is a strategy to provide a forum for questions like these.

...MANY TIMES STUDENTS WILL HAVE QUESTIONS THEY WOULD LIKE TO HAVE ANSWERED...

USES

Motivational Environment, Classroom Management

PROCEDURE

1. Decorate a box to put near the classroom door – label it "The Question Box."

2. Ask the students to put any questions they have in the box as they exit the classroom.

3. Collect the questions and either . . .

   • put an answer on them;

   • put a reference for the answer; or

- write on the question that it will be addressed as a part of the unit.

4. Post the results of step three on a special part of the wall or bulletin board that has been set aside for this purpose.

Grade Level: Elementary, Middle, High School

Time: On-going

Special Materials: Decorated box, Cards

Motivational Standards: Safe

3.32 QUESTION WALLS

PURPOSE

To provide a forum for student questions.

DESCRIPTION

This strategy is very similar to *Question Boxes* in both purpose and procedures. The most obvious difference between the two is that in this strategy, the students post their questions visibly on the wall.

USES

Motivational Environment, Classroom Management

PROCEDURE

1. Label a large sheet of butcher paper with a phrase like "The Question Wall." Add decorative drawings, question marks, or sample questions to the paper.

2. Provide removable sticky notes (or 3 x 5 cards) on which students are to write their questions.

3. At the beginning of a unit, and throughout a unit, have the students post their questions on The Question Wall.

4. Provide time for students to post answers to other students' questions.

5. As the unit progresses, be certain to build in time for addressing questions from the wall where it is appropriate to do so.

6. When a student learns an answer to one of his/her questions, have him/her post the answer with the question.

7. At the conclusion of the unit, the students can put their questions and answers in their portfolio tracking their growth as self-directed learners.

Grade Level: Elementary, Middle, High School

Time: 10 minutes

Special Materials: Chart paper, removable self-stick notes or 3 x 5 cards and tape

Motivational Standards: Safe, Involving

Pluses: Block Schedules, Multiple Intelligences

QUICK TIP

3.33   RESPONSE OPPORTUNITIES

A response opportunity is an event that prompts the students to become mentally engaged and respond publicly in some way. Questions and prompts that engage the learners' minds help to maintain interest.

Avoid periods of more than ten minutes during which the students are not being asked to engage their minds and produce a response. Every few minutes, provide opportunities for the students to respond to a question or prompt. Asking questions of the whole class helps to keep the opportunities for each student frequent. Dignify all responses.

Examples:

"How many of you think that President Truman did the right thing in using the atomic bomb?"

"Let me see how many of you think that . . . "

"Let's see how many groups can come up with similar reasons that . . ."

Thanks to Dr. Raymond Wlodkowski for introducing us to this quick tip.

3.34 SITUATIONAL TEACHING (AN ADVANCED STRATEGY)

PURPOSE

To provide a teaching approach designed to promote self-direction.

DESCRIPTION

This is an approach to teaching in which the primary purpose is two-fold: 1) help students from where they are, and 2) help students become more self directed. Situational Teaching is adapted from the leadership model "Situational Leadership" developed by Dr. Ken Blanchard.

USES

Instruction

EXPLANATION

When students have a task to do, they are at one of four different possible stages in development. The levels are easiest to understand if you remember when you first learned how to perform a complex skill like bike riding.

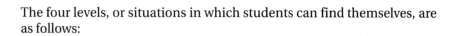

High Teacher Support | III | II
Low Teacher Support | IV | I

Low Teacher Direction   High Teacher Direction

The four levels, or situations in which students can find themselves, are as follows:

I. They have no knowledge or experience to tell them how to progress. Their confidence levels are okay because they have not experienced difficulty with the task. When students are at this level, they need a lot of direction, and when they get it they will just plow ahead. This is the first stage of development toward self-direction. When students are at stage I, provide lots of clear, step-by-step, effective direction/instruction. They don't need a lot of nurturing - just tons of guidance. As they see themselves progressing with your good guidance, they should be seeing enough evidence of progress to be highly motivating.

Can you remember what it was like when you first started learning to do something like bike riding? How did you feel? What did you need? What did you want? What didn't you need?

II. In stage II, the students have some knowledge and experience, but they are at an early stage of development and are prone to errors, wrong directions, and pitfalls. This level is called, "knowing just enough to be dangerous." Their confidence levels tend be low at this stage because they have just enough knowledge and experience to be making mistakes and having difficulty performing at the level of quality they desire. At this stage in a given situation, the student needs a lot of nurturing and support. The student continues to need a lot of clear, as easy as possible, step-by-step direction/instruction. It is essential that the direction/instruction be effective at providing successes at this stage.

This is not a good time to test, quiz, or use speed checks for accountability. Unfortunately, in our rush to cover the curriculum, this is precisely the point we tend to administer the "tests" for too many students. High levels of accountability are important, but at this point for students, the consequences can be devastating on their level of motivation. Assess the students' progress during this stage to facilitate instructional decisions, but hold off on using the assessments for accountability.

Remember when you were at stage II while learning to ride a bike? Did you discover it wasn't as easy as you thought? How important was the nurturing you received as you struggled? How important was the persistent, gentle, and effective instruction you continued to receive? What might have been the result without the strong and effective nurturing and instruction at this stage for you?

III. When the students reach stage III, which they will do if the traumas of stage II are addressed well by both the students and the teachers, the confidence begins to return. This is the level in the students' development with the given task/situation during which they begin to be ready for accountability. They still aren't totally sure of themselves during this stage, and their confidence will be variable.

As they progress, it is important to continue to provide an abundance of nurturing, but the amount of direction/instruction needs to diminish and become intermittent. This is when they need to experiment, be supported when they fail, and be helped to get back on track. If stages I and II have been addressed well, then this is when we take care to encourage and support self-direction.

Remember when you were at this stage with bike riding? You probably wanted to go around the block on your own. Sometimes you got in trouble and needed nurturing and more guidance, and sometimes you cried out, "Watch me!" and almost soared like a bird around the corner for an afternoon with your friends.

IV. Stage IV is the level at which the students are functioning at a self-directed level. During this stage, the skills and confidence are both high enough that very little direction and support are needed.

Remember when you finally got to stage IV with bike riding? What's necessary for most kids to reach this level? How does that pertain to a classroom?

PROCEDURE

1. Through your own experiences, familiarize yourself with the four stages of development (from knowing nothing to being self-directed with a given skill or ability).

2. Recognize that if a person is engaged in numerous different situations requiring learning/development at the same time, he/she is most likely at different stages with each of them.

3. Recognize that if there are 25 students in a classroom about to learn or use a given ability, those students may very well be in different stages.

4. Familiarize your students with the four levels of development addressed by the Situational Teaching model. Work with them until everyone can provide numerous examples from past and present experiences that show they understand the different levels and the needs within each one.

5. With each new situation addressed in the classroom, have the students identify at which level they are. (This is to be private between you and each student.) Be prepared to provide varying levels of support and direction/instruction for the four different groups of students that will become apparent to you.

The Situational Teaching model leads to the belief that the most unfair thing we can do as teachers is to treat all students alike in a given situation. The success of the model is based on the communication and trust that needs to exist between all concerned.

Grade Level: Elementary, Middle, High School

Time: On-going

Special Materials: None

Motivational Standards: Safe, Successful, Enabling

QUICK TIP

3.35 START ON TIME

Whether every student is on time or not, some almost always are. Honor their timeliness by starting on time, show your respect for those who made it on time, and demonstrate your commitment to honor your agreements. The following are some possible ways to begin on time in various situations:

- "I would like to thank all of you for being on time. Let's begin by ..."

- "A number of students are not here yet because ... While we wait, let's take advantage of this time by ..."

- "A number of students are obviously not here, but it is time to start, so let's begin by ..."

- "A number of students must still be trying to find the room. Since it's the first day, we'll give them five more minutes to find us. In the meantime, let's use this time to learn at least three things about the person sitting across from you."

- "Thanks for being here on time. I'll be with you in two minutes, but in the mean time, please begin with ..."

3.36 STRETCH BREAKS TO REENERGIZE THE STUDENTS

QUICK TIP

At least once every 30 minutes provide an opportunity for students to get up and move. As a minimum, you can ask them to stand up and down on their toes while breathing deeply. You'll be amazed at the difference in your students' energy levels when you do this.

3.37 TEACHING POSITIONS

QUICK TIP

You can facilitate students' learning by establishing special places for yourself in the classroom based on what you're doing at the time. The location of these places is not as important as how consistent you are in using them. Pick and consistently use special places for:

- obtaining the attention of the students in your classroom;

- giving information; and

- engaging in or facilitating dialog with the students.

3.38 VALUE-ADDED ACTIVITIES

Whenever you are faced with a break, lunch, assembly, or any event that will probably result in several or more students returning late, use a value added activity. Value-Added Activities do exactly what the name implies – they add value to learning. They help to add increased clarity, depth, or breadth for those students who make it back on time, but they are not something that will throw off the lesson if a student misses them. Examples could be activities in this series such as *Similes* and *Quotes & Cartoons*. Typically a value-added activity is one that promotes meaningful discussion about the topic but does NOT present new information or skills.

QUICK TIP

3.39 VISUALS

15 QUICK TIPS FOR OVERHEAD TRANSPARENCIES, COMPUTER PROJECTIONS & FLIP CHARTS

QUICK TIP

Almost nothing can frustrate and demotivate students faster than visuals they can't see or understand quickly. The following are quick tips for keeping your visuals effective.

1. For text, use dark color pens like blue, black, or purple. Resist the temptation to use bright colors for anything other than highlight marks.

2. Use colors like red, orange, or green to highlight points by circling or underlining.

3. Keep your visuals simple:

    • Show major points only;

    • Use six or fewer words per line; and

    • Use five or fewer lines.

4. Don't crowd things – keep lots of white space.

5. Be certain the students with the most limited vision can see visuals clearly from anywhere in the room.

    • Use large print (avoid cursive) or large point sizes.

    • Check overheads by putting them on the floor and reading them while standing - they should be very easy for you to see and read.

    • Use fonts that have distinctly different shapes for letters so that they don't appear too similar from a distance - when in doubt, check the a's, e's, and o's.

6. Vary colors only to visually differentiate points or, on flip charts, alternate between two dark colors for each point.

7. Use colors consistently. Once color is used with a concept, continue to use that color with that concept only.

8. Avoid using the backgrounds that many commercial software packages provide for transparencies. In many cases, these are effective on television, but distracting on transparencies.

9. Raise the screen as high as possible and consider putting it in a front corner.

10. Use only the top half to two-thirds of a transparency.

11. Use both upper and lower case letters. Avoid using all capitals because they are harder to read.

12. Use pictures or icons whenever possible. They convey ideas very quickly.

13. Put main ideas on charts or posters if they are to be referred to throughout a lesson or unit. (See *Concepts on the Wall*.)

14. Build complex graphics as they are discussed with the students. Complex graphics, when suddenly put in front of a learner, can create visual overload and mental shut down. When building the complex graphic, draw the overall outline first, then fill in the pieces.

15. When using an LCD panel, make sure you use a projector with a brightness level that meets the manufacturer's specifications for the size of audience and screen. Typically, LCD panels do not work well with audiences over 50 to 100 (maximum) depending on the projector and screen size. Changes in technology are gradually fixing these problems.

3.40 VISUAL POINTERS

QUICK TIP

Take advantage of the power of color and/or shape coordination to show what and how information, concepts, or steps in a process connect.

Included with this quick tip are numerous shapes that can be used as pointers or bullets when teaching with overhead transparencies. Use these pages to make overhead transparencies on films of different colors.

Before teaching with these pointers/bullets, be certain you have enough of the different shapes you MAY need in as many different colors as you MAY need to adhere to the following:

- Always use the same color/shapes for the pointers/bullets you are using for thoughts you want the students to see as connected.

- Use different colors/shapes for thoughts you want the students to see as separate thoughts.

CAUTION

Just as color and shapes can be used to enhance learning, if we aren't careful, they also can cause incorrect learning and confusion.

Transparency Pointers

Create colored transparencies of this page. Then cut out the pointers for use on an overhead projector. Be careful to use colors consistently.

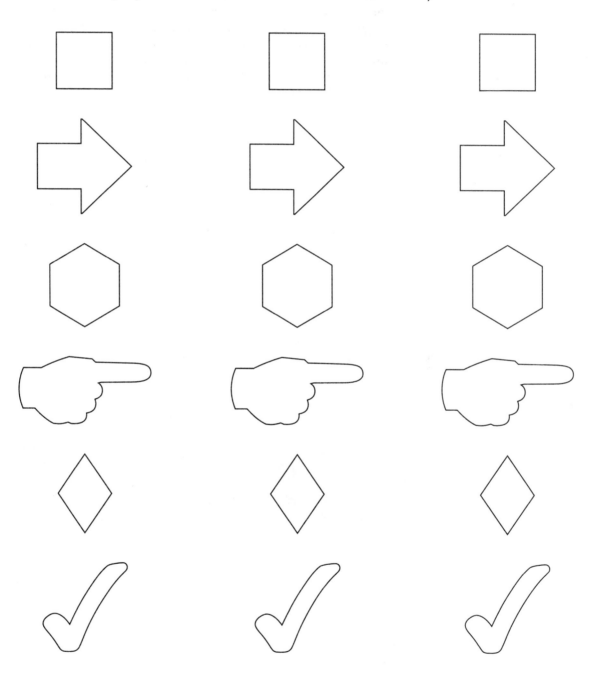

QUICK TIP

3.41 WAIT UNTIL READY

When we first work with a group of students, they usually give us their attention as soon as we ask for it. This doesn't always last. However, there is one trick to help the situation.

Make sure that when you ask the students to give you their attention, you are absolutely ready to begin and that you do begin from your "beginning position" as soon as you have their attention. (See *Teaching Positions.*) Too often we slip into old habits of asking for our students' attention before we are absolutely ready. The result is that the students learn very quickly that when we're asking for their attention, we don't really mean it because we are not actually ready to begin.

CHAPTER 4

BUILDING KNOWLEDGE AND UNDERSTANDING

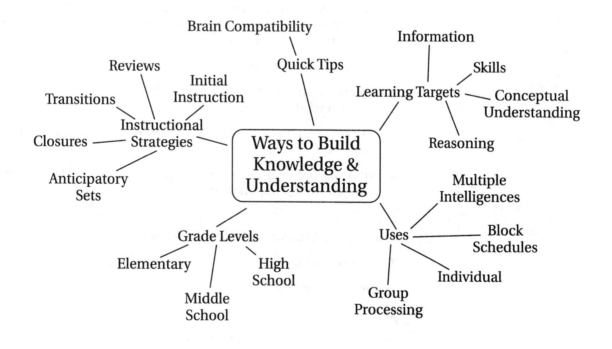

4.1   BACK TRACKS

PURPOSE

To facilitate collaborative reviewing to start or close a lesson.

DESCRIPTION

This is a great collaborative and high energy activity for reviewing a previous lesson before picking up where you left off.

INSTRUCTIONAL USES

Anticipatory Set, Closure, Transition

TARGETED LEARNING

Information, Conceptual Understanding

PROCEDURE

1. Give the students 2-3 minutes to individually review their materials from the day before and select what they consider to be the three most important concepts.

2. Have them form triads.

3. Have each student in the triads share her reflections for two minutes with her triad members.

4. Ask each triad to determine the three most important concepts from the day before.

5. Have one person from each triad report to the whole class one of their three most important concepts.

Grade Level: Elementary, Middle, High School

Time: 10 minutes

Special Materials: None

Motivational Standards: Enabling

Pluses: Block Schedules, Group Processing

4.2 BEFORE AND AFTER PICTURES

PURPOSE

To promote deeper thinking while checking for understanding.

DESCRIPTION

This activity provides a quick closure to a unit, lesson, or instructional approach while providing the teacher with a "picture" of the learning that has occurred.

INSTRUCTIONAL USES

Closure, Transition

TARGETED LEARNING

Information

PROCEDURE

1. Have each student fold a piece of standard sized paper in half. Give them the choice of working either length or width wise.

2. Ask the students to open the paper and label one half "before" and the other half "after."

3. Give the students about 5-10 minutes to draw before and after pictures for a particular lesson, unit, or instructional approach, that convey:

   • how they felt before and after;

   • what they knew or believed before and after; or

   • what they thought before and what they wondered about after.

4. Ask the students to explain their drawings in small groups, post them on the wall or collect them, and provide non-judgmental feedback for each one.

VARIATION

Allow the students to write rather than draw their responses.

Grade Level: Elementary, Middle, High School

Time: 10 minutes

Special Materials: None

Motivational Standards: Enabling

Pluses: Block Schedules, Group Processing, Multiple Intelligences

4.3 BEGINNING, MIDDLE, & END

PURPOSE

To provide an anticipatory set while also providing the students and the teacher with a means of tracking learning within a unit.

DESCRIPTION

In this activity, the students record their learning of specific objectives throughout a unit.

INSTRUCTIONAL USES

Anticipatory Set, Closure, Review, Instruction, Transition

TARGETED LEARNING

Information, Skills

PROCEDURE

Beginning, Middle, & End

Topics	Beginning	Middle	End

1. Determine the 3-5 topics or concepts that you consider most significant within the unit.

2. Provide the students with a full sheet of paper that is set up like the graph on the following page.

3. In the "Topic" column, have the students list the significant topics or concepts you have identified.

4. At the beginning of the unit, have the students write in the "BEGINNING" column the most significant knowledge they already have for each topic or concept. (It is not necessary to restrict this to the lower levels of Bloom's Taxonomy.)

5. At an appropriate time during the unit, have the students record their most significant knowledge with respect to each concept in the column labeled "MIDDLE."

6. Repeat at the end of the unit.

Grade Level: Elementary, Middle, High School

Time: 5, 15, 30 Minutes

Special Materials: Printed page with appropriately labeled columns

Motivational Standards: Involving, Valuable, Enabling

Pluses: Block Schedules, Group Processing, Multiple Intelligences

Beginning, Middle, & End

Topics	Beginning	Middle	End

4.4 BYSTANDER HELP

PURPOSE

To provide a fun writing exercise for learning and reviewing important concepts.

DESCRIPTION

In order to explain or teach a concept to someone else, one must have a clear understanding of the concept itself. This exercise facilitates students evaluating their understanding of a concept and translating their thoughts into clear, simple, and concrete terms by using an interesting writing exercise.

INSTRUCTIONAL USES

Review, Instruction

TARGETED LEARNING

Conceptual Understanding

PROCEDURE

1. Write a short passage, including dialog between two small children, about a specific concept or topic. The conversation between the two children should include some correct and incorrect information about the topic. (Make it humorous.)

2. After reading the paragraph, instruct the students to identify the correct and incorrect information.

3. Have students respond in writing (as if they are an intervening third person), directly to the young children, explaining the concept in a very simple and clear manner (so a five year old could understand).

4. Encourage the students to be creative and make their responses fun.

VARIATION

Include a word bank of specific terms that should be included in the student response to the young children.

Grade Level: Middle School

Time: 15-30 minutes

Special Materials: None

Motivational Standards: Valuable

Pluses: Block Schedules, Group Processing, Multiple Intelligences

Thanks to Jim Burton for contributing this strategy.

4.5 CAROUSEL GRAFFITI

PURPOSE

To facilitate the generation of ideas or processing of concepts.

DESCRIPTION

This lively activity gets students moving around while gathering and contributing to one another's thoughts. In groups of 3-5, the students physically move and respond to a series of open-ended questions. Use this activity whenever there are several questions or complex concepts in which you want all students to contribute and to build complex understanding.

INSTRUCTIONAL USES

Anticipatory Set, Closure, Review, Instruction

TARGETED LEARNING

Information, Conceptual Understanding

PROCEDURE

1. Record each question you wish the students to address with a separate sheet of chart paper. The questions should be open-ended and thought provoking. Generate one question for every three to five students.

   Example Questions:

   "How would things be different if Columbus had discovered California?"

   "How do elephants benefit from their enormous ears?"

   "What might be the result of . . . ?"

   "What could happen if . . . ?"

   "What would be the benefits of . . . ?"

2. Tape the pieces of chart paper on the wall so that they are spread out around the room.

3. Divide the students into groups. The number of groups must equal the number of questions to be answered.

4. Assign each group of students to one of the questions as its "home base" and starting point.

5. Give the groups a reasonable amount of time to respond to their questions (usually one to five minutes). Have the groups record their responses on their chart paper using a broad, felt-tip pen.

6. At the end of the allotted time, ask the groups to rotate one position to a new question and begin responding to it. Have the groups add their new responses to those already there.

7. Continue the group rotation, gradually shortening the amount of time they have with each question.

8. When the groups have each returned to their original question, change their task. Ask them to summarize the responses recorded by the various groups, and then to report their summary to the class.

HINT:

Increase accountability and involvement by giving each group its own different colored pen to carry with them and use as they work their way around the room.

Grade Level: *Elementary, Middle, High School*

Time: *15-30 minutes*

Special Materials: *Chart paper, markers*

Motivational Standards: *Involving/Enabling/Successful*

Pluses: *Block Schedules, Group Processing, Multiple Intelligences*

Many thanks to Dr. Raymond Wlodkowski and Dr. Margery Ginsberg of Boulder, Colorado for introducing us to this great strategy.

4.6   CARTOONS & QUOTES

PURPOSE

To provide a base for light and lively student processing of information.

DESCRIPTION

This is a powerful value-added strategy that uses cartoons and quotes to facilitate students engaging in discussions about the intended learning while also promoting conjecture, reflection, or prediction. Use this strategy when you want to devote 5 - 10 minutes to re-focusing and re-energizing the students.

INSTRUCTIONAL USES

Anticipatory Set, Closure, Review, Instruction, Transition

TARGETED LEARNING

Information

PROCEDURE

1. Develop a collection of quotes and/or cartoons that provoke thought.

2. Display a cartoon or quote that is interesting to the students. Enlarge it as much as possible and read it aloud if it is on an overhead projector.

3. Ask the students as individuals or in small groups to develop a statement regarding what the cartoon or quote could be conveying in connection to the intended content learning.

SAMPLE QUOTATIONS

"Change is the law of life. And those who look only to the past or the present are certain to miss the future."
— John F. Kennedy, 1963

"The greatest thing in the world is to know how to be self-sufficient."
— Michel de Montaigne, (1533-1592)

"Before you give somebody a piece of your mind, make sure you can get by with what you have left."
— Anonymous

> *"If you have built castles in the air, your work need not be lost; that is where they should be. Now put foundations under them."*
> — Henry David Thoreau, (1817-1862)

> *"An appeaser is one who feeds a crocodile - hoping it will eat him last."*
> — attributed to Winston Churchill, (1874-1965)

> *"Even if you're on the right track, you'll get run over if you just sit there."*
> —Will Rogers

> *"If in the last few years you haven't discarded a major opinion or acquired a new one, check your pulse."*
> — Gelett Burgess

Grade Level: Elementary, Middle, High School

Time: 5-10 minutes

Special Materials: Cartoons and/or Quotes

Motivational Standards: Valuable, Enabling

Pluses: Block Schedules, Group Processing, Multiple Intelligences

4.7   CHALLENGE ENVELOPES

PURPOSE

To facilitate review and/or higher level processing of a topic or concept.

DESCRIPTION

This activity is designed to provide students with opportunities to formulate challenging questions regarding a topic or concept and to be challenged by the questions of others.

INSTRUCTIONAL USES

Anticipatory Set, Closure, Review, Instruction

TARGETING LEARNING

Conceptual Understanding

PROCEDURE

1. Give each team of students an envelope.

2. Have each team write a challenge question on the front of its envelope – encourage higher level questions that have prompts like

   - What might be … ?

   - What could be … ?

   - What if … ?

3. Have each team generate the answer or criteria for a response and include a sample response, then put it in the envelope.

4. Scramble the envelopes, and have the teams rotate the envelopes through the class. When a team receives an envelope, the question is to be addressed and then checked against the answer or criteria in the envelope.

5. Have each team put its response to a question in its envelope when they are done and put it back into circulation.

6. As the envelopes begin to fill with responses, the teams are to compare their responses to the others that are in the envelopes.

VARIATION

This variation was shared by Rebecca Swanson: "I play stump the teacher. I ask the students to make up challenging questions to ask me. They have a lot of fun and get a good review at the same time."

Grade Level: Elementary, Middle, High School

Time: 30 minutes

Special Materials: Envelopes, 3 x 5 Cards

Motivational Standards: Enabling

Pluses: Block Schedules, Group Processing, Multiple Intelligences

4.8 CHALLENGE OF THE WEEK

Set aside time each week for a challenging question or problem that is interesting, requires complex thinking, and involves the use of important content. Strive to find challenges that connect the content to the world, and thus provide relevance.

Challenge the students to bring in "challenge problems for the class to work on."

QUICK TIP

4.9 CLASSIFIED LEARNING

PURPOSE

To help students build knowledge and understanding through classification.

DESCRIPTION

When students are asked to classify concepts, procedures, or things they need to analyze for essential characteristics or traits.

Note: the following procedure needs to be carefully modeled, taught, and practiced outside of the content area before it is used to enhance the learning of content concepts or skills. Also, the language should be simplified for younger students.

INSTRUCTIONAL USES

Instruction

TARGETED LEARNING

Information, Conceptual Understanding, Skills

PROCEDURE

1. Provide the students with an organizer to facilitate their efforts. This can be in the form of a matrix, a set of boxes, or a Venn diagram.

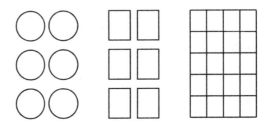

2. Either provide the students with a list of items to be classified or develop a list with them.

3. Determine one item in the list that appears to be significant enough to represent a "desired category."

4. Have the students select other items from the list that fit into the category.

5. Have the students develop the rules that determine membership in the category.

6. Have the students select the next item from the list that represents another major category.

7. Have the students continue until all the items are classified or until it becomes obvious that categories need to be combined or reconsidered.

8. Have the students continue until done.

9. Ask the students to prepare a summary showing the categories, the rules for inclusion, and any conclusions that can be drawn.

Grade Level: *Elementary, Middle, High School*

Time: *Varies*

Special Materials: *None*

Motivational Standards: *Involving, Enabling*

Pluses: *Block Schedules, Group Processing*

Classification

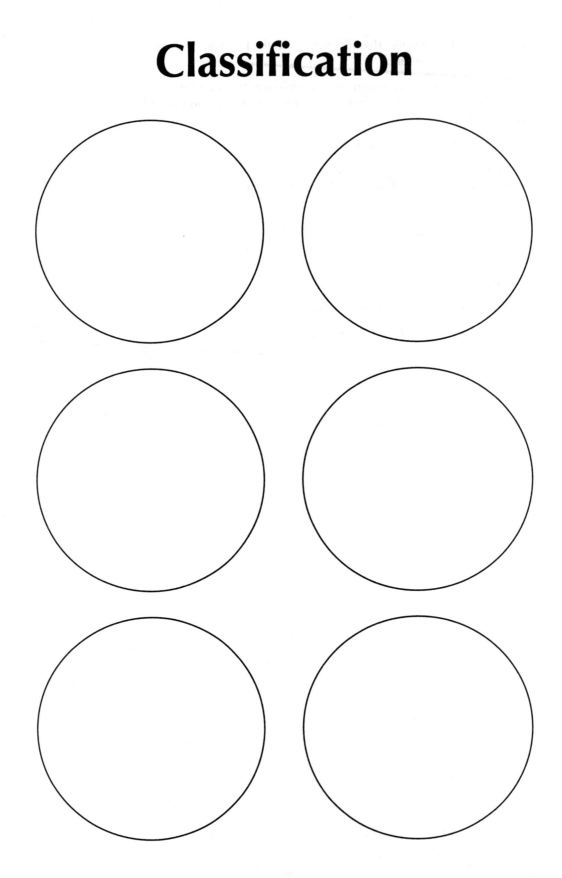

4.10   CLOSURE WITH SENSITIVITY

A closure activity that draws on many senses was shared with us in a workshop by Doug McPhee, the author of *Limitless Learning* (Zephyr Press, 1996). At the end of a lesson or unit, ask the following questions of the students:

QUICK TIP

> "What did you see?"

> "What did you hear?"

> "How did you feel?"

Doug also suggests that these questions can be followed with the question:

> "Where does it fit?"

4.11   CLUMPING

PURPOSE

To provide for quick reviews before beginning a lesson.

DESCRIPTION

In this activity, the students generate lists of "items" that fit a given concept or topic.

INSTRUCTIONAL USES

Anticipatory Set, Closure, Review

TARGETED LEARNING

Conceptual Understanding, Information

PROCEDURE

1.   Begin the activity by identifying the specific "clump" (group) of items with which the students are to work.

2.   After identifying the clump, write 3 to 5 items that fall into this group on the board, on an overhead transparency, or a piece of flip-chart paper.

3.   Ask students to add to the list, and continue to write the ideas until students have run out of offerings.

Examples:

    A. The "clump" we are working with is <u>adjectives</u> that end in "<u>FUL</u>."

       Such as: beauti<u>ful</u>, bounti<u>ful</u>, and grate<u>ful</u>.

       What are additional ones you can add to the list?"

    B. The list we are building today deals with <u>dietary considerations</u>.

       Such as: grams, carbohydrates, and fats.

       What additional items might you add to the list?

4. When students are familiar with the strategy, it can be "up-leveled" by **NOT** identifying the specific "clump" before the activity begins. Start the activity by listing 3 to 5 items and then inviting the students to add to the list. By conducting the activity in this way, the students must first look for the similarities and differences in the examples in order to identify the characteristics they have in common and then deciding into which topic or concept they fall. This requires more complex thinking and is great for developing the idea of "concept" and the ability to compare and contrast.

Grade Level: *Elementary, Middle*

Time: *5 minutes*

Special Materials: *None*

Motivational Standards: *Enabling*

Pluses: *Block Schedules, Group Processing*

4.12   CONCEPT ATTAINMENT

PURPOSE

To facilitate students gaining new concepts.

DESCRIPTION

Concepts can be introduced by showing students a number of examples that represent a concept and a number that don't, and then having the students develop the characteristics or attributes of the concept.

INSTRUCTIONAL USES

Instruction

TARGETED LEARNING

Conceptual Understanding

PROCEDURE

1. Provide a number of examples that clearly contain the essential characteristics of the concept being introduced. Also provide the students with a number of examples that are similar but do not contain the essential characteristics (non-examples - they may contain some essential characteristics of the targeted concept, but they mostly contain characteristics that make them examples of what the concept is not). Ask the students to project what they believe are the defining characteristics.

2. Provide more clearly identified examples and non-examples (each of which is clearly labeled.) Ask the students to check their hypothesis from step 1 and revise as necessary.

3. Repeat Step 2 until all (or at least most of) the student groups are able to correctly identify the defining characteristics of the concept.

4. Direct the students to identify examples and non-examples of the concept. Ask them to be certain they can defend their choices based on the defining characteristics.

5. Have the students share their examples and non-examples with the class.

6. Ask the students to develop oral or written descriptions of the concept. They may use pictures, drawings, rhymes, or charts to support their descriptions, but they must at least include the defining characteristics.

Adapted from numerous models including those presented in *Teacher's Manual for Dimensions of Learning* (Marzano, ASCD, 1992), *A Study of Thinking* (Wiley, 1956), and *The High Performance Toolbox* (Peak Learning Systems, 1997).

Grade Level: Elementary, Middle, High School

Time: Varies

Special Materials: None

Motivational Standards: Involving, Enabling

Pluses: Block Schedules, Group Processing

4.13   CONCEPT MAPS

PURPOSE

To reinforce learning and increase depth and breadth of understanding.

DESCRIPTION

This is an excellent strategy to structure students' review and organization of information and major concepts taught.

INSTRUCTIONAL USES

Anticipatory Set, Closure, Review, Instruction

TARGETED LEARNING

Information, Skills, Conceptual Understanding, Reasoning

PROCEDURE

1.   Divide the students into groups of two to three.

2.   Provide each group with a large sheet of butcher paper.

3.   Have the students start in the center by writing a major concept inside a circle.

4.   Ask the students to print rather than to use cursive – it's easier to read and it's better for memory.

5.   Have the students either take turns or work together to develop the next steps in their maps. Tell them to branch out from the main concept to its supporting concepts and to explain the connections (See diagram).

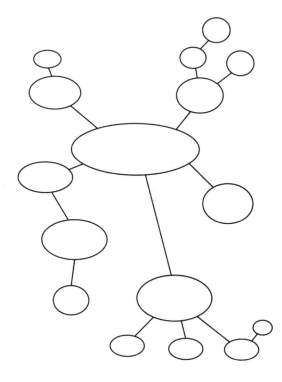

6. Encourage the students to use key words in identifying the concepts.

7. Have the students use lines and colors to show the connections.

8. Ask each group to share their concept map with another group or the whole class.

VARIATION

Have the students include connections and applications from outside of school.

Grade Level: Elementary, Middle, High School

Time: 20 minutes and up (varies with scope)

Special Materials: Chart Paper, Markers, Tape

Motivational Standards: Enabling, Involving

Pluses: Block Schedules, Group Processing, Multiple Intelligences

4.14 CONCEPTUAL T-CHARTS

PURPOSE

To help students develop understanding of a concept of which they already have some knowledge.

DESCRIPTION

The students use T-charts to help develop their understanding of a targeted concept. On the left side of the T-chart, they record all those characteristics that fit the concept. On the right side of the T-chart, they record all those characteristics that don't fit the concept but are connected to it. The students can be encouraged through prompts and facilitation to go as far in discovering the nuances of a concept as desired.

INSTRUCTIONAL USES

Anticipatory Set, Closure, Review, Instruction, Transition

TARGETED LEARNING

Information, Conceptual Understanding, Skills, Reasoning

PROCEDURE

1. Have the students draw a T-chart that fills a full size sheet of paper.

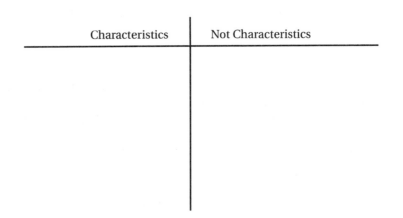

2. Ask them to label the left side with a specific statement regarding what's true about the concept. Examples for the left side of the T-chart include:

   • "characteristics *animals* have in common;"

   • "*exponential function* characteristics;"

- *"behaviors* of students in groups in which they love to work hard and contribute;"

- "characteristics of *characters in Charles Dickens' writings*;" and

- "*wave* characteristics."

3. Have them label the right side of the T-chart with characteristics that don't fit and yet are connected to the concept. Examples include:

   - "characteristics that make something not an animal;"

   - "characteristics of functions that are not exponential;"

   - "*behaviors* of students in groups in which they lose interest and tend not to contribute;"

   - "characteristics of characters developed by authors other than Charles Dickens;" and

   - "characteristics of particles."

4. Ask the student teams (or individuals) to complete their T-charts with specifics. Encourage them to dig for nuances that really help to clarify the concept.

5. Have the groups share the contents of their T-charts while you or a designated student records on the overhead or chart paper.

6. Ask the students as individuals, and then as teams, to draw any conclusions and make any generalizations they can that are supported by the group findings.

7. If applicable, ask the students to determine how they can use their discoveries.

HINT

Have the students work in teams of two to five to complete their T-charts and draw conclusions. However, be certain to manage the strategy so individuals brainstorm in writing before any open team brainstorming.

Grade Level: Elementary, Middle, High School

Time: Varies with Concept

Special Materials: T-chart

Motivational Standards: Involving, Enabling

Pluses: Block Schedules, Group Processing

4.15   CONNECTION WEBS

PURPOSE

To help students find and develop connections within and between concepts or topics.

DESCRIPTION

In this strategy, the students create a web of yarn showing important connections they are to be learning.

When students are faced with learning a large amount of information, it can be very challenging. One way to help students learn information in a meaningful way is to have them find as many connections and interconnections as they can. An added plus is that students continue to develop their thinking skills in the process. This strategy is particularly useful when working with literary characters and/or complex topics and concepts from areas such as history, music, mathematics, economics, and the sciences.

INSTRUCTIONAL USES

Closure, Review, Instruction

TARGETED LEARNING

Information

PROCEDURE

1. One or two days before the activity is to take place, have students randomly select names of characters in the literary piece being studied or the topics or concepts being addressed. Their task is to review the material and to become very familiar with their character/concept.

2. On the day of the activity, divide students into smaller groups and have them arrange themselves in a circle. (The size of the groups depends on the number of characters/concepts assigned. If the number is large, fewer groups are required. If the selection has very few characters, more groups will allow for more student interaction.) Have each student make a name plate with his/her concept/character's name on it and place this card in clear view.

3. Hand one of the students a ball of twine and have him/her explain a relationship he/she has with one of the other characters/concepts. When the student is finished, have him/her hold on to the end of the twine and toss the ball of string to the student representing the new character/concept.

4. The character/concept now holding the ball of twine tells about a relationship he/she has with another character/concept, holds on to the string, and tosses the ball to that character/concept. (Students should be instructed not to deal with the same character/concept who just gave them the twine unless it is absolutely necessary. This will help to create the tangible effect of an intricate web). At this time, tell the students not to let go of their string until the activity has been closed.

5. Have students continue to build their "web of relationships" until they have run out of ideas.

6. To close the activity, have the students representing various characters/concepts pull their strings one at a time. If the character/concept is a major one, many students will feel the tension; if the character/concept is minor, very few others will feel the tension. Finally, have students summarize what they have learned about the characters/concepts and the interconnections between them.

Grade Level: Elementary, Middle, High School

Time: 20 minutes

Special Materials: String, yarn or twine, paper for nameplate, markers

Motivational Standards: Enabling, Involving

Pluses: Block Schedules, Group Processing, Multiple Intelligences

4.16 CON-VENN-TION

PURPOSE

To provide an anticipatory set, closure, or review by having the students share and compare knowledge and perspectives on a given topic.

DESCRIPTION

In this strategy, groups of students develop Venn diagrams containing knowledge/perspectives regarding a given topic. It is used before beginning instruction on a unit in which the students may be very diverse in their prior knowledge. It provides a fun way for the students to bring forward their background knowledge while learning from one another. It also lets you gain a clear picture of the prior learning that each student has.

INSTRUCTIONAL USES

Anticipatory Set, Closure, Review

TARGETED LEARNING

Information

PROCEDURE

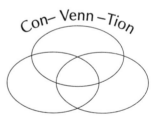

1. Develop guidelines that the students can use to determine their knowledge level (quite knowledgeable, know some, know a little) with respect to the topic.

2. Have the students form groups of three in which all the students are at about the same knowledge level.

3. Assign or have students select roles of timekeeper, process keeper, and materials officer.

4. Provide each group with at least 24 large removable "sticky" notes or 3 x 5 cards and a large sheet of butcher or flip chart paper.

5. Ask the students to individually write the 5-8 most significant points they know with respect to the given topic on the "sticky" notes or 3 x 5 cards – one idea per "sticky" note or card. Tell them that each point needs to be clear and precise enough to be meaningful and usable to a reader. (Allow five minutes for steps five and six.)

6. Ask each student to write one thing they wonder about each topic on a separate card.

7. Have the members of each group share with each other their points and questions while sorting them into piles of:

   • all 3 students had it,

- student 1 and student 2 had it,

- student 2 and student 3 had it,

- student 1 and student 3 had it,

- only student 1 had it,

- only student 2 had it, or

- only student 3 had it.

8.   Have the students post their points and questions on a giant Venn diagram based on who had what.

9.   Ask the groups to prepare a one minute presentation to the class in which they will present their common points and most burning question.

Grade Level: *Elementary, Middle, High School*

Time: *20 - 40 minutes*

Special Materials: *"Sticky notes" or 3 x 5 cards, chart paper, tape*

Motivational Standards: *Involving*

Pluses: *Block Schedules, Group Processing, Multiple Intelligences*

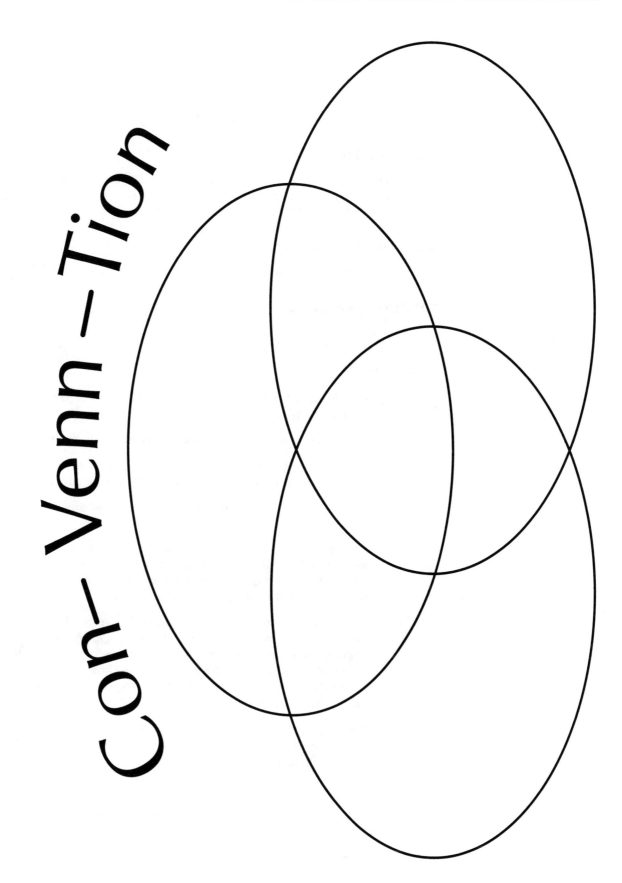

Con–Venn–Tion

4.17 CROSSWORDS

PURPOSE

To provide an active closure or anticipatory set for a lesson or unit.

DESCRIPTION

This strategy uses the concept of a crossword puzzle as the basis for students processing information, topics, or concepts. It works well with students as individuals or in small groups.

INSTRUCTIONAL USES

Anticipatory Set, Closure, Review

TARGETED LEARNING

Information

PROCEDURE

1. Clearly identify the significant information, topics, or concepts for students to review.

2. Decide if you want the students to work individually or in groups.

3. Remind the students of the area of study and ask them to help you brainstorm the important information, topics, or concepts.

4. Suggest or add any important ones that the students have not generated.

5. Cut and combine topics or concepts to reduce the list of targeted words to what you consider to be a reasonable number for the time available, the area of study, and the need to preserve novelty. (It is a good idea to limit the topics to no more than 10.)

6. Tell the students to use the words identified in step five for the words in a crossword puzzle they are to develop. Ask each student or group to also pick at least two other targeted words to include in their puzzles. Challenge the students to see how many of the targeted words they can use. (Do NOT give extra credit or points for those who go beyond the targeted words plus two.)

7. Ask the students to develop a crossword puzzle that they could use to teach or check someone's knowledge of the area of study. Remind them to develop good questions for each of the targeted pieces of information, topics, or concepts.

8. Have each crossword puzzle worked by several different groups or individuals as a means of evaluation for refinements.

HINT

The students' processing of the information comes through the development of the questions.

Grade Level: Elementary, Middle, High School

Time: 15-20 minutes

Special Materials: Chart paper or poster board, markers, tape

Motivational Standards: Enabling

Pluses: Block Schedules, Group Processing, Multiple Intelligences

4.18   CROSSWORD REVIEW

PURPOSE

To identify and/or review the main points of a given topic.

DESCRIPTION

Using an important word as a prompt, the students build meaningful phrases or sentences that convey either what they already know or what they have learned about a significant topic.

INSTRUCTIONAL USES

Anticipatory Set, Closure, Review, Transition

TARGETED LEARNING

Information

PROCEDURE

1. Give each student group a piece of chart paper, and have them write the teacher chosen prompt word vertically down the left side of the paper.

2. For each letter of the prompt word, have students write a significant phrase or sentence that begins with that specific letter.

3. Encourage the groups to address all main ideas.

4. Upon completion, post each chart and have the students compare and contrast them looking for such things as repeated ideas, concepts they agree are significant but didn't identify, etcetera.

Example Prompt Word = Goal

G oals are what we want to achieve.
O nly do what will help reach the goal.
A ll goals need to be specific.
L imit to 3-5 major goals.

HINTS

This activity can also be done with small groups. Students need to be reminded that the sentences or phrases do not have to be grammatically correct - "The Big Idea" is the most important focus.

Grade Level: Elementary, Middle, High School

Time: 10-15 minutes

Special Materials: Chart paper, Markers, Tape

Motivational Standards: Enabling, Involving

Pluses: Block Schedules, Group Processing, Multiple Intelligences

4.19 DEPICTIONS & REPRESENTATIONS

PURPOSE

To review or process information through visual interpretation.

DESCRIPTION

Many students learn best and retain information longer when they have a chance to create some form of visual interpretation/representation of the learning. This activity is designed to create a context to support that.

INSTRUCTIONAL USES

Anticipatory Set, Closure, Review, Instruction

TARGETED LEARNING

Information, Conceptual Understanding

PROCEDURE

1. Determine the concept or connections that need to be developed and/or reinforced.

2. Develop at least one depiction of that concept or those connections, label it well, develop an explanation of it, and share your work with the students.

3. With the class, develop standards for good depictions using yours and any others that can be found as models.

4. Ask the students to create their own depictions and explanations according to the standards that you have developed together.

5. Have the students peer assess their efforts and refine as needed.

6. Have each student present his/her depiction and explanation to the class.

VARIATION

Encourage the students to utilize other art forms such as music to enhance their depictions/representations — and refer to their work as "representations."

Grade Level: Elementary, Middle, High School

Time: 30-45 minutes & up (varies with scope)

Special Materials: Chart paper or construction paper, markers, pens, scissors, glue or paste, magazines, tape

Motivational Standards: Enabling

Pluses: Block Schedules, Group Processing, Multiple Intelligences

4.20   DISTRIBUTED PRACTICE

PURPOSE

To improve students' long-term retention of important information, skills, and concepts.

DESCRIPTION

Distributed practice is a strategy for effectively using review based on research regarding memory curves. Over the years, research has shown that when students are asked to review (practice what has already been learned) with gradually expanding intervals, they remember their learning longer. Distributed practice is review within each unit of instruction that is based on an incremental and iterative bringing forward of essential learnings from previous units. In addition to increasing student retention of important learnings, this strategy can be used to gradually expand the students' level of understanding and sophistication of skill usage.

INSTRUCTIONAL USES

Review

TARGETED LEARNING

Information, Skills, Reasoning, Conceptual Understanding

PROCEDURE

1. Beginning with your first unit, select those learnings that are most important to remember and/or to be further developed incrementally. These selections are what will be used for distributed practice in future units.

2. Plan exercises and activities in each unit throughout the year that have the students practicing and/or extending the knowledge and skills targeted from previous units for distributed practice.

3. Include assessment questions in each unit that check for student progress with what has been used for distributed practice.

4. Based on assessment results, plan another round of "distributed practice" for the next unit or for the unit following that one.

5. Continue the "distributed practice" pattern with expanding intervals between each practice.

Grade Level: *Elementary, Middle, High School*

Time: *Varies*

Special Materials: *None*

Motivational Standards: *Successful, Enabling*

4.21 DOOR PASSES

PURPOSE

To check the levels of knowledge or understanding regarding concepts taught during a lesson.

DESCRIPTION

This is a simple and quick strategy that promotes students reflecting over their learning while providing you with a valuable last check of their learning. The basic idea is that at the end of a lesson the students are asked to write their specific reflections on a piece of paper. These pieces of paper become the students' passes out the classroom door.

INSTRUCTIONAL USES

Anticipatory Set, Closure, Transition

TARGETED LEARNING

Information, Conceptual Understanding, Skills

PROCEDURE

1. At the end of the lesson and about five minutes before the students are to leave the classroom, ask them to take out a piece of paper to use as their "pass out the door."

2. Ask the students to describe or explain the major concepts from the lesson.

3. Have the students hand you their door passes as they leave the classroom.

4. Use the students' responses as a basis for planning the next lesson.

HINT

Encourage pictures, rhymes and metaphors.

The prompts in chapter six work well for this strategy.

Grade Level: Elementary, Middle, High School

Time: 5 minutes

Special Materials: Index cards, printed door passes, or scraps of paper

Motivational Standards: Enabling

Pluses: Block Schedules, Group Processing, Multiple Intelligences

Special thanks to Dr. Kit Marshall for introducing this strategy to us.

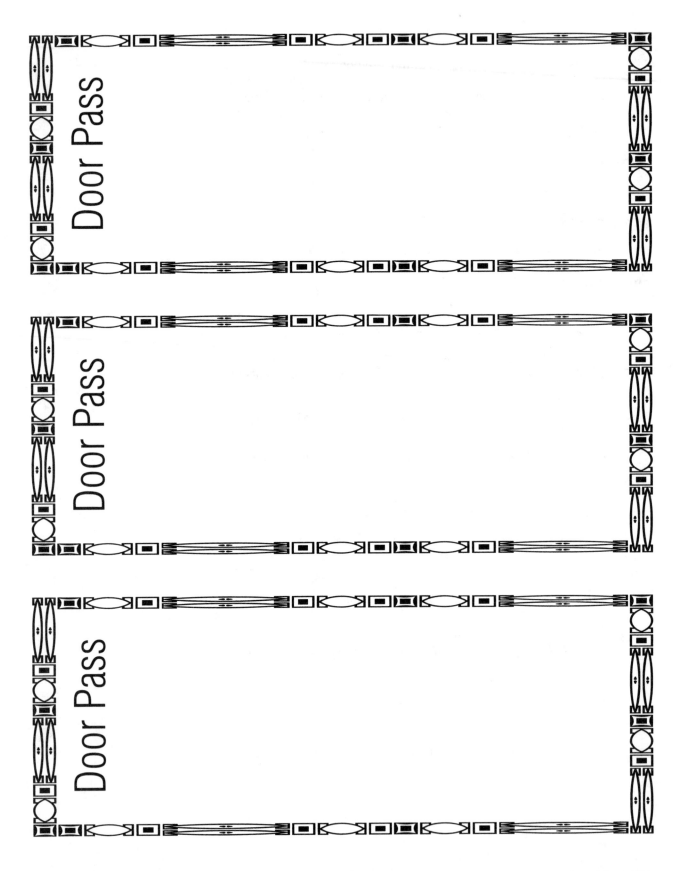

Door Pass

Door Pass

Door Pass

4.22 DUMP, CLUMP, & LUMP

PURPOSE

To provide a step by step process for organizing thinking and facilitating learning of new and difficult information.

DESCRIPTION

This is a great strategy to use when the students are faced with learning new and difficult information. It provides students with a process for organizing their prior knowledge and making projections. Depending on the subject matter, this strategy could utilize up to a full class period. Each of the three phases can be worked through in one long session or broken up into three separate sessions.

INSTRUCTIONAL USES

Anticipatory Set, Closure, Review, Instruction

TARGETED LEARNING

Information, Skills, Conceptual Understanding, Reasoning

PROCEDURE

1. "Dump" Stage (presenting) - Have students develop a list of words, items, or new information to connect the learning(s) (i.e. a list of items one would see in the year 1695, a list of issues a political candidate needs to consider before running for office, etcetera.)

2. "Clump" Stage (grouping) - Ask students to compare and contrast the items on their list. Then, ask them to group the items and label the groups.

3. "Lump" Stage (integrating) - Have students merge groups and hypothesize, form questions, or make predictions. They are to write statements supporting and/or refuting their findings. Have the students share their ideas with the class either verbally or on chart paper that is posted.

Grade Level: Elementary, Middle, High School

Time: 20 minutes

Special Materials: None

Motivational Standards: Enabling

Pluses: Block Schedules, Group Processing, Multiple Intelligences

Thanks to Richard Strong of Hanson, Silver, and Strong.

4.23 ENCAPSULATING SENTENCES

PURPOSE

This activity is designed to promote reviewing and integrating information provided in a lesson.

DESCRIPTION

In this strategy, the students are asked to develop a sentence that best expresses what they have learned or know about a given concept or topic.

INSTRUCTIONAL USES

Anticipatory Set, Closure, Transition

TARGETED LEARNING

Information, Reasoning

PROCEDURE

1. Ask the learners to write one sentence that *best summarizes or encapsulates what they consider to be the most important* aspects of the lesson.

2. Ask them to make their sentences clear and specific – discourage them from just listing topics or concepts.

3. Either post the sentences or select three to four to read aloud.

Grade Level: Middle, High School

Time: 5 minutes

Special Materials: None

Motivational Standards: Enabling

Pluses: Block Schedules, Group Processing

4.24   ERROR ANALYSIS

PURPOSE

To develop editing and error analysis skills.

INSTRUCTIONAL USES

Instruction

TARGETED LEARNING

Information, Skills, Conceptual Understanding, Reasoning

PROCEDURE

1. Prepare a word, statement, problem, paragraph, report, piece of music, or picture for display that contains errors from small to conceptual.

2. Have the students work individually or in groups to locate or determine the errors in mechanics, thinking, skills, or judgment.

3. Ask the students to compare their findings and develop corrections.

EXAMPLE ERROR TYPES:

- misspelled words
- grammatically incorrect sentences
- incorrect paragraph structures
- inaccurate information
- improper skill usage
- illogical conclusions

Grade Level: Elementary, Middle, High School

Time: 10-20 minutes

Special Materials: None

Motivational Standards: Enabling

Pluses: Block Schedules, Group Processing

Thanks to Lyn Reville for contributing the idea for this strategy.

4.25   FAIRY TALES, SONGS, & POEMS

PURPOSE

To facilitate learning through multiple intelligences.

DESCRIPTION

This activity is designed to allow the students to integrate the learning into a format that appeals to their particular style.

INSTRUCTIONAL USES

Review, Instruction

TARGETED LEARNING

Information, Skills, Conceptual Understanding, Reasoning

PROCEDURE

1. Identify the significant concepts or skills the students will be learning.

2. Tell the students they will be rewriting a commonly known fairy tale, song, or poem so that it relates to the significant aspects of the concepts they are about to learn.

3. Teach the concepts.

4. Ask the students to work as individuals or in small groups to quickly adapt their selected fairy tale, song, or poem so that it relates to the identified significant concepts or skills. An example that could be developed by students is *The Three Little Quadratics (Pigs)*.

ASK THE STUDENTS TO . . . ADAPT THEIR SELECTED FAIRY TALE, SONG, OR POEM SO THAT IT RELATES TO THE IDENTIFIED SIGNIFICANT CONCEPTS OR SKILLS

Grade Level: Elementary, Middle, High School

Time: 30 minutes

Special Materials: Books with fairy tales, poems, and songs

Motivational Standards: Enabling

Pluses: Block Schedules, Group Processing, Multiple Intelligences

4.26 FINAL COUNTDOWN

PURPOSE

To cause reflection, evaluation, and integration of learning.

DESCRIPTION

As educators, we know the importance that reflection plays in the learning process. Therefore, we need to create frequent and structured activities that provide learners with a framework for reflection.

INSTRUCTIONAL USES

Anticipatory Set, Closure, Transition

TARGETED LEARNING

Information

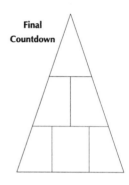

Final
Countdown

PROCEDURE

1. Ask students to individually reflect over the learnings they have had concerning a given topic.

2. In their "learning logs," or on a sheet of paper, have students respond to the following prompts:

   • What are the **three** most important things you have learned today? Or, what are the three most important things you have learned during this unit?

   • What are **two** questions you would still like answered?

   • What is **one** way what you have learned connects with what you knew before?

3. Periodically, collect the student logs in order to read and respond to students' reflections.

HINT

Encourage pictures, rhymes, and metaphors.

Grade Level: Elementary, Middle, High School

Time: 5-10 minutes

Special Materials: None

Motivational Standards: Enabling

Pluses: Block Schedules, Group Processing, Multiple Intelligences

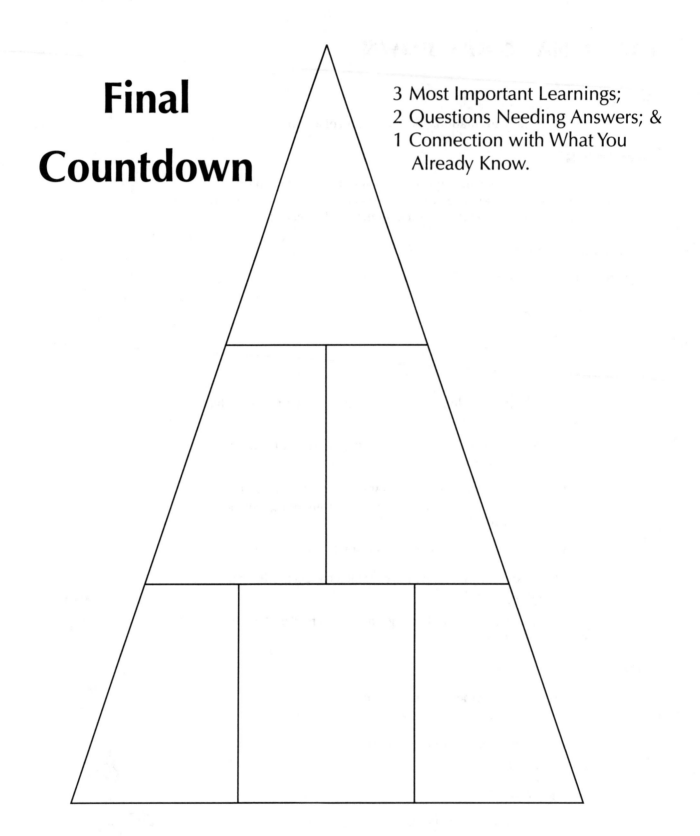

Final Countdown

3 Most Important Learnings;
2 Questions Needing Answers; &
1 Connection with What You Already Know.

4.27 FIND A MODEL

PURPOSE

To increase the depth of understanding of concepts.

DESCRIPTION

Students' understanding of mathematical and scientific concepts is increased whenever they work with actual models. In this strategy, the students are asked to find or build examples or models that show aspects of the concepts they are working with in school. They are then asked to present their findings or models to the class.

INSTRUCTIONAL USES

Review, Instruction

TARGETED LEARNING

Conceptual Understanding

EXAMPLE CONCEPTS TO BE USED

1. Fractional relationships including improper fractions

2. Decimal representation of numbers

3. Reflective properties of conic cross sections

4. Relationships between pressure, temperature, and volume

5. Relationship between the area of triangles and rectangles

HINTS

Present several example findings or models to the class before asking students to develop and present their own.

Ask the students to practice their presentation with their parents or guardians.

Be prepared to help those students who become frustrated when asked to do something that is more open ended than they are used to doing.

> *Grade Level:* Elementary, Middle, High School
>
> *Time:* Varies; 2-3 days (outside of classroom assignment)
>
> *Special Materials:* None
>
> *Motivational Standards:* Enabling, Involving
>
> *Pluses:* Block Schedules, Group Processing, Multiple Intelligences

Thanks to Barb McCoy for contributing this strategy.

4.28   FIVE STARS AND A WISH

PURPOSE

To prepare the students for a lesson by having them reflect over what they know about the topic.

DESCRIPTION

This is a quick lesson opener that can give you a sense of where the students are while warming up their minds.

INSTRUCTIONAL USES

Anticipatory Set, Transition

TARGETED LEARNING

Information, Skills

PROCEDURE

1. Ask the students to write on a sheet of paper (or a 3 x 5 card) five things they know about the topic you are about to teach. When naming the topic, be general enough that there is room for the students to surface prior knowledge.

2. Ask the students to share in small groups or whole groups what they wrote.

3. Ask the students to each write one thing they don't know, a question they have, or something that troubles them with respect to the topic.

4. Collect their responses to number three either orally or by picking up their papers.

5. Explain to the students how during the lesson (or unit) they will find responses to the questions or concerns they surfaced in step three.

Grade Level: *Elementary, Middle, High School*

Time: *15 minutes*

Special Materials: *None*

Motivational Standards: *Enabling*

Pluses: *Block Schedules, Group Processing*

4.29 FOUR SQUARE

PURPOSE

To provide for mental processing of information or concepts.

DESCRIPTION

This activity helps provide the students with choices as to how to draw closure to a lesson.

INSTRUCTIONAL USES

Closure, Review, Transition

TARGETED LEARNING

Information, Skills, Conceptual Understanding

PROCEDURE

1. Prepare a diagram like the following.

2. Ask the students to do one of the four activities provided in the above matrix or concept to convey the major points of a targeted topic or concept.

Grade Level: *Middle, High School*

Time: *10 minutes*

Special Materials: *4 Square Handout*

Motivational Standards: *Enabling*

Pluses: *Block Schedules, Group Processing, Multiple Intelligences*

Draw a Picture	**Write a Paragraph**
Compose a Song or Rap	**Make a List**

4.30 FOUR - TWO - ONE

PURPOSE

To empower students by providing an opportunity to reflect on, evaluate, and integrate their learning.

DESCRIPTION

This strategy uses learning partners or small teams to foster in-depth reflection and integration of significant information.

INSTRUCTIONAL USES

Anticipatory Set, Closure, Review, Transition

TARGETED LEARNING

Information, Skills, Conceptual Understanding, Reasoning

PROCEDURE

Ask the students to:

1. Individually generate four words that capture the most important aspects of the learning experience.

2. Share, with learning partners or in small teams, their four words and compile a list of the words they have in common. From this list, determine two words that they agree capture the most important aspects.

3. Determine the 1 word or Big Idea that best represents the most important learning of the experience.

4. Share the various lists generated by their group in order for the whole class to make as many learning connections as possible.

VARIATION

Ask the students to generate phrases or sentences.

EXTENSION

Ask each student to write a sentence that conveys the most significant learning(s).

Grade Level: *Elementary, Middle, High School*

Time: *10-15 minutes*

Special Materials: *None*

Motivational Standards: *Enabling*

Pluses: *Block Schedules, Group Processing*

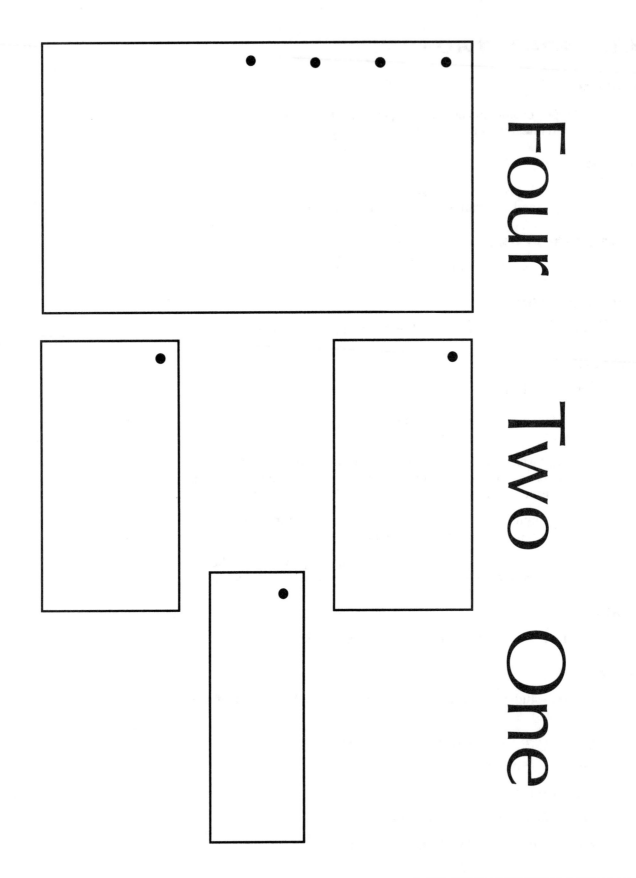

4.31 GOAL WALL

PURPOSE

To facilitate students preparing their minds for a given unit and to provide you with insight as to how to ensure a unit is interesting to the students.

DESCRIPTION

A goal wall is a portion of a wall that is set aside for the students to post what they would like to learn about a given topic.

INSTRUCTIONAL USES

Anticipatory Set, Motivational Environment

TARGETED LEARNING

Information, Skills, Conceptual Understanding

PROCEDURE

1. Ask the students to record on a 3 x 5 card a question about the upcoming topic they would be interested in having answered (their learning goals). Request that the students put their names on their cards.

2. Have the students share their questions within groups of five students.

3. Direct the students within each group to determine the categories into which the questions fall. Have the groups share their categories and facilitate a conversation to develop a common set of categories.

4. Ask the students to post their questions on the Goal Wall in sections that have been labeled with the categories identified in step 3.

5. Review and address the questions as you teach the unit.

6. Have each student record an answer to his/her question by the end of the unit and place his/her goal card in his/her Journal, Learning Log, or Growth Portfolio.

Grade Level: Elementary, Middle, High School

Time: 25 minutes

Special Materials: 3 x 5 cards or sheets of paper.

Motivational Standards: Valuable, Involving, Successful, Enabling

Pluses: Block Schedules, Group Processing

QUICK TIP

4.32   HOLIDAY DECORATIONS

Ask the students to make decorations that can be hung in the classroom (or some other public place) during the holiday season. Direct the students to design the decorations so that they convey some significant information or concepts from your curriculum.

4.33   INSIDE OUT
(CIRCULAR QUESTIONING)

PURPOSE

To reinforce critical thinking skills and to provide additional processing of content.

DESCRIPTION

This activity creates a context where students can process information by either designing questions or formulating answers and discussing the results. It helps to reinforce the content while at the same time allowing students to do what they love most - TALK!

INSTRUCTIONAL USES

Anticipatory Set, Closure, Review, Transition

TARGETED LEARNING

Information

PROCEDURE

1. After reading a novel or studying a body of information, ask students in the class to write two questions for each designated category. The categories vary depending on the content, but they need to involve critical thinking skills.

    Examples:

    Cause and effect: What did it mean when … ?

    Clarification: Why did he or she do that?

    Multiple cause: What else might have caused it?

Alternative action: What could be done to change the situation?

Prediction: What might happen if ...?

2. Students are then divided into two groups. One group forms an inner circle and the second group forms an outer circle with all chairs facing inward. The outside circle is the group that asks the questions, and the inside circle is the group that responds to the questions. During the time set aside for this activity, it is critical that the students have the opportunity at least once to experience being in each role. When it is time to switch, the students should literally get up and exchange seats in order to maintain the kinetic format of what happens in each position.

3. Once the circles are set, a volunteer from the outside circle asks the first question. A volunteer from the inside circle responds to the question. When this person is finished, anyone else in the inside circle can add information, clarify what has been said, or politely disagree and explain why. If someone in the outer circle wants to add information, they must do it in the form of a question.

   Note: You may want to use a student checker to record the number of contributions.

4. The process continues until all questions have been asked and clarified.

Grade Level: Middle, High School

Time: 30 minutes

Special Materials: None

Motivational Standards: Enabling

Pluses: Block Schedules, Group Processing

4.34 INTO, THROUGH, AND BEYOND

PURPOSE

To assess students' prior knowledge regarding an upcoming unit/topic and facilitate them building on it through connections, extensions, and projections.

DESCRIPTION

This strategy uses a three phase questioning process:

1. What do I already know about the topic; how does it all connect; and what questions do I have?

2. What have I learned so far and how does it all connect and begin to answer my questions?

3. What do I now know; what questions do I have; and how does it all connect?

INSTRUCTIONAL USES

Anticipatory Set, Closure, Transition

TARGETED LEARNING

Information, Skills, Conceptual Understanding

PROCEDURE

The "into the learning" phase

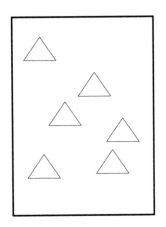

1. Ask students to draw six triangles on a piece of notebook paper. (The triangles should be 1.5 to 2 inches at the base.) Students should place the triangles randomly all over the paper, leaving a lot of space between the triangles.

2. Ask the students to write the name of the topic at the top of their papers.

3. Have the students, individually or in groups, determine the three to six most important things they already know about the topic.

4. Direct the students to write one significant thing from step three in each triangle. If they have triangles that are blank, have them put one question about the topic in each of the remaining triangles.

5. Ask the students to draw lines connecting those triangles for which the content of the triangles conceptually connects. (Some teachers skip this step.)

6. Have the students get into pairs or groups of three to four and share their ideas, making note of the ones that they have in common. (Consider asking the groups to report these common ideas to the whole class.)

7. Have students keep their papers for later use, or collect them.

The "through the learning" phase – after a substantial amount of learning has occurred.

1. Ask students to use their "Into, Through, and Beyond" for the next phase of the process. Have them draw six circles in between and around the triangles, randomly.

2. Have the students record one significant new learning in each of the six circles.

3. Ask the students to correct any errors of which they are now aware in the triangles .

4. Have students draw lines showing the conceptual connections between the contents of the triangles and the circles.

5. Have students share their new learnings and connections with a partner or small group. (Some teachers like to have each group report out to the whole class).

6. Again, have students keep their papers for later use, or collect them.

Note: This phase of the strategy can be done numerous times, depending on the complexity or duration of the lesson or unit.

The "beyond the learning phase" to be done at the completion of the unit.

1. Ask students to use their "Into, Through, and Beyond" for the final phase of the process. Have them draw three squares in between and around the circles and triangles, randomly.

2. In the squares, have the students write one thing they would like to continue exploring and their two most significant learnings.

3. Have students draw lines showing the conceptual connections between the contents of the squares, circles, and triangles.

4. Direct the students to share their new ideas and connections with partners or small groups. Again, some teachers like to ask the groups to share this with the whole class.

5. Have students save their *Into, Through, and Beyond* graphic for review later on in the year.

Grade Level: Elementary, Middle, High School

Time: On-going, 5-20 minutes each time it is done in class

Special Materials: None

Motivational Standards: Involving, Enabling

Pluses: Block Schedules, Group Processing

Thanks to Dr. Kit Marshall for introducing us to this strategy.

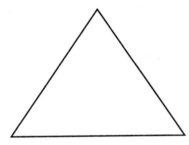

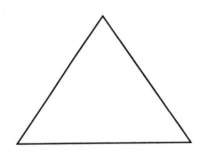

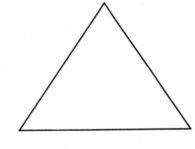

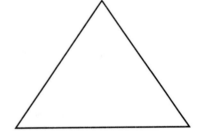

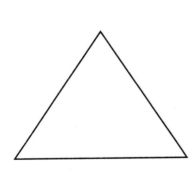

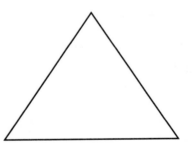

4.35   KNOWLEDGE PROBES

PURPOSE

To foster complex thinking, review of content, and increase motivation through student involvement in their education.

DESCRIPTION

Whenever teachers make up the test questions or prompts (prompts are expressions like, "explain the cause of ....") , they're the ones who get to do the complex thinking and heavy duty review, and hone their skills in determining which parts of the content are the most important. In this strategy, the students develop test questions and the acceptable answers or criteria for the answers to questions that are more open-ended.

INSTRUCTIONAL USES

Review, Instruction

TARGETED LEARNING

Information

PROCEDURE

1. Teach the students about the different levels that questions/ prompts can represent (information, understanding, projecting, etcetera). This can be done by providing students with example questions that they can answer and having them determine the categories that the questions/prompts represent. Be certain the questions contain several examples from desired levels such as . . .

    • What is …? What was …? Who is or was? What does? (Questions asking for factual information that can be memorized.)

    • Describe …   Explain …

    • Find the area of … when given …

    • Solve the following …

    • What might happen if …? What might have been the result if …?

2. Ask the students to generate a predetermined number of questions or prompts for each level.

3. For each question/prompt generated, ask the students to determine the appropriate answers or criteria for the answers.

4. Have the students turn in what they produce, duplicate it, and distribute copies to the class. Use what they have produced as a

source for quiz questions – providing they are aligned with your curriculum and assessments.

> *Grade Level:* *Middle, High School*
>
> *Time:* *1 hour*
>
> *Special Materials:* *None*
>
> *Motivational Standards:* *Involving*
>
> *Pluses:* *Block Schedules, Group Processing*

4.36   K-W-L

PURPOSE

To provide a vehicle for students to surface prior knowledge and questions regarding a targeted learning, and to then build on new learning and prior knowledge.

DESCRIPTION

K-W-L is a strategy that is used to facilitate students' learning by building on their prior knowledge and generating interest in the topic. According to our research, it was first developed by Donna Ogle (1986).

INSTRUCTIONAL USES

Anticipatory Set, Transition

TARGETED LEARNING

Information, Skills

PROCEDURE

1. Identify and clarify the specific topic or concept to be the focus for the learning.

2. Ask the students to identify what they think they already **Know** about the topic.

    An example from Social Studies: Before the class begins a unit on the Election Systems in The United States, ask the students to identify everything they already know about how people are elected to public office. (This can be done individually or in groups.)

3. Have the students identify what they **Want** to know about the topic. These may be questions they have had for a while or questions that arose as they were identifying what they already know.

> Example student questions for the topic of political elections: What is the Electoral College? What role does it play in determining the winner of the presidential campaign? How can a person be elected president while losing the election?

4. Proceed to teach the unit using best instructional practices. Perhaps engage the students in researching the given topic/concept through reading, classroom instruction, interviewing, etc.

5. Using the questions posed in the second step as a focus for the learning, the students are to identify what they have **Learned** as they work through the unit.

Grade Level: Elementary, Middle, High School

Time: Variable

Special Materials: None

Motivational Standards: Enabling

Pluses: Block Schedules, Group Processing

4.37 LEARNING THROUGH INDUCTIVE THINKING

PURPOSE

To help the students build knowledge and understanding through the use of induction.

DESCRIPTION

In this strategy, the students are asked to analyze concepts, things, or procedures in order to determine the details and then to make generalizations. For example, at an elementary level, they may analyze a number of photographs and conclude that they all represent people having fun in winter.

Note: the following procedure needs to be carefully modeled, taught, and practiced outside of the content area before it is used to enhance the learning of content concepts or skills. Also, the language should be simplified for younger students.

INSTRUCTIONAL USES

Instruction

TARGETED LEARNING

Information, Conceptual Understanding, Skills, Reasoning

PROCEDURE

1. Teach and "think aloud" an induction example.

2. Present your students with the item(s) or situation(s) with which they are to use induction.

3. Ask the students to determine as many specifics (details) from each item or situation – looking in particular for those that may fit a pattern.

4. Direct the students to make a generalization that is supported by the results of step 3.

5. Have the students check and modify their generalization by testing against more analysis of the item(s) or situation(s).

VARIATION 1

1. Present (or develop with the students) a list of factual information regarding a concept. (Examples include steps in solving lots of types of equations or economic effects after numerous wars.)

2. Ask the students to develop generalizations or draw conclusions based on the facts presented.

3. Ask them to check their generalizations and conclusions against other examples or research supported patterns.

VARIATION 2

1. After having studied trends, theories, or connected events, ask the students to predict what will most likely occur next or what the chances (probability) are that something will occur (in a general sense).

2. Ask the students to develop a logical argument to support their claims.

Grade Level: Elementary, Middle, High School

Time: Varies

Special Materials: None

Motivational Standards: Involving, Enabling

Pluses: Block Schedules, Group Processing

4.38 MASTERY LEARNING

PURPOSE

To increase student accountability for learning essential objectives and to enhance motivation through evidence of mastery.

DESCRIPTION

Often times, because we have too much to do and not enough time, we shortcut how we do things. This seems to be the case many times in teaching. At home with our children, we tend to teach and re-teach until our children ultimately have acquired intended skills to the level we desire. At school, we typically work very hard to teach, give a test, and move on – even though some students, if not many, have not yet met our standard.

Mastery Learning was formalized through the work of Benjamin Bloom, James Block, and Thomas Guskey. Since its early development, significant research has been gathered to support its use and effectiveness as a model. However, in recent years, it has come under heavy criticism because it has been associated with inappropriate or ineffective approaches to its implementation.

INSTRUCTIONAL USES

Instruction

TARGETED LEARNING

Information, Conceptual Understanding, Skills, Reasoning

PROCEDURE

1. Clearly identify the learning objectives for a given unit. Identify precisely what students need to be able to show you they know and can do in order to have met those objectives.

2. Use your best available teaching practices to teach the learning objectives.

3. Administer a formative test to determine whether or not each student has met the objectives yet.

4. For the students who have met the objectives, provide some type of enriching experience (research of their choice).

5. For the students who have not yet met the objectives, provide an alternative form of instruction for them to boost their level of achievement – then administer a second test, different but parallel in difficulty and focus.

6. If students retest one or more times, allow them to keep their highest scores. This way, the students learn that taking risks and hard work can have definite advantages.

Grade Level: *Elementary, Middle, High School*

Special Materials: *None*

Motivational Standards: *Successful*

Pluses: *Block Schedules*

We would like to thank Benjamin Bloom, James Block, and Thomas Guskey for their research and roles in developing this concept.

4.39   MEMORY HOOKS

PURPOSE

To facilitate students remembering topics throughout a lesson or unit.

DESCRIPTION

This is a very old method of helping the memory by creating associations. It requires the use of several common objects that can be used as memory hooks for the associations. Possible hooks are a toy car, a doll, keys, a plant, a toy truck, a pencil or pen, scissors, a ruler, or a drinking cup. The hooks need to be such that you can hold them up for all to see, rich and complex enough for varied associations, and a part of the common experiences of all the students.

INSTRUCTIONAL USES

Anticipatory Set, Closure, Instruction, Transition

TARGETED LEARNING

Information, Skills

PROCEDURE

1. Teach a "logical" chunk of content for 5 to 11 minutes.

2. Tell the students you are going to help them remember what has

been taught by asking them to associate it with a common object.

3. Hold up one of the objects for all to see and describe it to the students (or ask a student to describe it). Remind them that they are to form associations with it.

4. If this type of thinking is new or developmentally challenging for the students, provide an example of an association for them.

5. Ask each student to quickly jot down an association by completing the sentence,

    "(the targeted learning) is like (the object) because . . ."

6. Ask the students to share their association with a neighbor or with the class.

HINT

Encourage diverse associations. In fact, after the students feel comfortable with finding associations, ask them to discuss the nature of the associations and why different people might be forming different types of associations. Be careful to show equal appreciation for all associations.

Grade Level: Elementary, Middle, High School

Time: 5 minutes

Special Materials: Small interesting, unique objects or pictures

Motivational Standards: Enabling

Pluses: Block Schedules, Group Processing, Multiple Intelligences

Thanks to Rob and Kathy Bocchino of Baldwinsville, New York for introducing us to this strategy.

4.40 MIX AND MATCH

PURPOSE

To promote the development of complete sentences as well as the identification of relationships between concepts.

DESCRIPTION

In this activity, the students are to find and express a relationship between two concepts.

INSTRUCTIONAL USES

Anticipatory Set, Closure, Transition

TARGETED LEARNING

Information, Conceptual Understanding

PROCEDURE

The teacher begins the activity by selecting two concepts that are related in some way and calling them out to the class. The students then use the two concepts in a complete sentence that conveys a relationship between them. Student responses can be gathered in several ways: taking volunteers, going round-robin around the room, calling on the first student and then having that student call on the next, etcetera.

Examples:

A. **Fire/Air** — "Mix and Match" = "Fire is used to heat the air in a hot air balloon, thus causing it to rise from the ground."

B. **Trains/West** — "Mix and Match" = "The speed at which the West was settled was greatly increased by the expanded train system."

Grade Level: *Elementary, Middle*

Time: *10 minutes*

Special Materials: *None*

Motivational Standards: *Enabling*

Pluses: *Block Schedules, Group Processing*

4.41 MUSEUMS

PURPOSE

To either bring forward the collective knowledge in a classroom or to provide for a comprehensive group review.

DESCRIPTION

This activity is powerful for bringing out knowledge from around the classroom or for reviewing at the end of a unit. The basic idea is that each group of students will create "museum-like" displays that present information or concepts in a logical manner regarding a specific, targeted topic.

Use this museum activity when you are certain that all the students have some pre-existing knowledge regarding the focus of the museum.

INSTRUCTIONAL USES

Anticipatory Set, Closure, Review, Instruction

TARGETED LEARNING

Information, Skills

PROCEDURE

1. Determine and share with the students the topic that is to be the focus of all their museum displays.

2. Divide the class into groups of five to seven students each.

3. Make certain that each group has at least eight large removable sticky notes or 3 x 5 cards for each person in the group.

4. Explain to the students that they will be working in groups to create and share a mock museum display.

5. If the activity is being used to launch instruction, let the students know they will be gaining a great deal of information from one another.

6. Tell the students they will be engaged in a multiple step activity with lots of starting and stopping. Remind the students to wait for the signals.

7. Be certain the students know and have practiced with the signals for starting and stopping.

8. Tell the students that for the first phase of the activity they are to work as individuals.

9. Tell them that when you say "go," they will have four to eight minutes

to write all the significant thoughts, information, procedures, etcetera about the predetermined topic on the cards with only one per card. (Deliberately set a specific time between four and eight minutes that will rush everyone and will not be enough time for most.) Tell them to begin.

10. Monitor carefully. Advise the students when they have 30 seconds remaining. Say "stop" precisely on time – let them know that everyone ran out of time.

11. Tell them that in the next phase they are to share their ideas. (Assign roles as needed). Advise them that each person is to share everything that he/she has recorded on cards or removable sticky notes.

12. As ideas are shared and patterns begin to develop, have the students organize all the ideas.

13. Ask them to appropriately label each category of ideas they have developed, and to prepare everything to be shared with other groups. (Clarify this if needed.) Give them a very tight time period— eight minutes is typically good.

14. If the time you've given is appropriate, none of the groups will be done. It's now time to negotiate for an additional amount of time.

15. Give the groups ten seconds to decide among themselves how many minutes they need. Have each group report out loud. Pick a time about in the middle and give them that amount of time.

17. Adjust time as necessary – no more than an additional minute should be needed.

18. Give the groups ten seconds to pick a "docent" – the person whose role it is to teach the students from other groups about what is in his/her museum. Tell the students that the docents will stay with their own museums to explain them to others while the rest of the group is to roam to the other museums to gather information.

19. Determine a time period that will allow the "roamers" to visit at most two other museums. This limited time forces the members of each group to develop a plan for making sure they can get the information from all the museums. Give them 30 seconds to plan.

20. Tell them to go out and learn from the other museums. Make sure the docents stay behind to teach. Hold to your time limit.

21. At the end of the roaming time, give them a short time (usually about three to five minutes) to report back anything new that they have learned while roaming and to add to and refine their museums accordingly.

22. Give the groups four to five minutes to develop clear and complete statements of the three most significant points contained in each of their museums.

23. Have each group pick a reporter.

186

24. One at a time, have the reporters stand and share ONE of their three most significant points in a way that doesn't repeat what other groups have said.

Grade Level: *Elementary, Middle, High School*

Time: *45 minutes*

Special Materials: *Chart paper, large post-it notes or 3 x 5 cards, tape*

Motivational Standards: *Enabling, Involving*

Pluses: *Block Schedules, Group Processing, Multiple Intelligences*

4.42 NOTE TO A FRIEND

PURPOSE

To increase depth of understanding of concepts and skills through writing.

DESCRIPTION

Research clearly shows people learn information better and retain it longer when they describe or explain it to someone else. This strategy has the students doing exactly that through "writing a note to a fictitious friend."

INSTRUCTIONAL USES

Review, Instruction

TARGETED LEARNING

Information, Skills, Reasoning, Conceptual Understanding

PROCEDURE

1. Tell the students to pretend a friend has been absent from class and they are going to describe "the learning" that their friend has missed in the form of a friendly letter.

2. Describe to the students the major parts of a friendly letter. Also emphasize the importance of clarity, precision, accuracy, depth and breadth.

3. Share with students the major topics or skills that need to be described in the letter.

4. Have students create their own ideas regarding effective ways to communicate with text, diagrams, and/or pictures.

5. Next, have the students share the rough drafts of their "letters" to check for clarity and errors.

6. Check the effectiveness of the students' final drafts by having students who are not in the course or grade level read the letters for understanding.

HINT

Encourage Students to be creative and have fun.

Grade Level: Elementary, Middle, High School

Time: 2 days and up (outside the classroom assignment-varies with scope)

Special Materials: None

Motivational Standards: Enabling

Pluses: Block Schedules, Group Processing, Multiple Intelligences

Special thanks to Jim Ludington and Spence Rogers for this strategy.

4.43 ONE - TWO REVIEW

PURPOSE

To provide an active closure or anticipatory set for a lesson or unit.

DESCRIPTION

This is a structured, quick, and interactive way to have the students bring previous learning forward to use as a foundation for new learning. It is also valuable as a means of promoting processing of new learning and facilitating shifts from short-term to long-term memory. This activity is designed to work best with the students in pairs.

INSTRUCTIONAL USES

Anticipatory Set, Closure, Review

TARGETED LEARNING

Information, Skills

PROCEDURE

1. Clearly identify a targeted topic that you wish the students to review or process.

2. Have the students find a partner.

3. Ask the students in each partner team to determine which one of them will serve as *partner one* and which one will serve *as partner two.*

4. Tell the students that when you give the signal to start, either partner one or two is to tell the other partner everything he or she can remember about the targeted topic for a period of three minutes.

5. Tell the students the targeted topic.

6. Before beginning the partner activity, give them two minutes to individually jot down everything they can about the targeted topic.

7. Tell the students that the partner that is listening will be asked to do something at the conclusion of the sharing.

8. Direct that either partner one or partner two begin sharing.

9. After three minutes, ask for their attention.

10. Ask the partners that were assigned to listen to share with the class something they heard that they thought was particularly important and why.

Grade Level: Elementary, Middle, High School

Time: 5-10 minutes

Special Materials: None

Motivational Standards: Enabling

Pluses: Block Schedules, Group Processing, Multiple Intelligences

Special thanks to Pat Wolfe for introducing us to this strategy.

QUICK TIP

4.44 OUT-OF-THE-BOX METAPHORS

Creativity occurs when we get out of the box and look at things differently. As an interesting, and sometimes humorous, sponge activity ask the students to create outlandish metaphors or similes. For example, Complete the following and be prepared to support your statement, "Metal is most like cotton candy because . . ." Another example is, "The westward expansion was most like a tree because . . ."

4.45 PROBE FOR UNDERSTANDING

PURPOSE

To promote deeper thinking while checking for understanding.

DESCRIPTION

So often students provide a quick answer that falls short of all they know or understand. This activity, when done with sensitivity, encourages students to think more deeply. It also provides the teacher with a clearer picture of what the students know or understand.

INSTRUCTIONAL USES

Instruction, Review

TARGETED LEARNING

Information, Conceptual Understanding, Skills

PROCEDURE

1. Create situations in which the students provide you with a response to a prompt regarding something with depth. For example, you might ask students studying the history of the Americas, "How would it be different today if Christopher Columbus had discovered California?"

2. After receiving a response from a student or a group of students, probe further (gently) with probes such as …

   • Can you tell me more about that?

   • Who might have benefited from …?

   • What else can you tell us?

• What might be some of the advantages of that?

• Can you help me to understand what you're saying?

• What might be the cause of that?

Grade Level: Elementary, Middle, High School

Time: Variable

Special Materials: None

Motivational Standards: Successful, Enabling

4.46   PROBLEM SOLVING WITH D²E³

PURPOSE

To facilitate students learning a problem solving process.

DESCRIPTION

D²E³ is an acronym for a complex problem solving process taught by this strategy.

INSTRUCTIONAL USES

Instruction

TARGETED LEARNING

Reasoning

PROCEDURE

1. Determine and Clarify – in the first step of the process, the students are asked to determine precisely what the problem is and bring clarity to it by determining its probable causes, the limitations or constraints on solutions, issues that surround the problem, and signs or symptoms of the problem.

2. Develop Options – in this step, the students are first asked to develop possible options for solutions without criticisms or challenges, and then they are asked to refine and expand their options.

3. Evaluate Options – have the students evaluate their possible solutions in light of the limitations and constraints determined in the first step of the process.

4. Engage in Implementing the Best Solution – in step four of the

process, the students are to actively engage in implementing their best solution.

5. Evaluate and Refine – have the students review, evaluate, and develop refinements to their problem solving skills used throughout steps 1 through 4.

Grade Level: Elementary, Middle, High School

Time: Varies

Special Materials: None

Motivational Standards: Enabling

Pluses: Block Schedules, Group Processing

4.47   PROBLEM SOLVING WITH POWER

PURPOSE

To facilitate students learning a problem solving process.

DESCRIPTION

POWER is an acronym for a problem solving process taught by this strategy. The process is first modeled and then applied with guided practice.

INSTRUCTIONAL USES

Instruction

TARGETED LEARNING

Reasoning

PROCEDURE

1. Share with the students a problematic situation with which they all can identify. (This situation needs to be "low stakes" and "high interest" for the students. An example: Many students have insufficient funds for all they wish to purchase.)

2. Tell the students that their task is to develop a viable solution to this situation through the use of a formal problem solving process.

3. On the board, an overhead, or a piece of chart paper, write the letters P O W E R vertically down the left side. After each letter, write the step of the problem solving process for which each letter stands. Instruct the students to copy this information in their notebooks.

    P   Identify and clarify the **Problem**, gathering and organizing all relevant information.

    O   Determine the **Obstacles** and constraints and their relative weights.

    W   Determine several **Ways** for solving the problem (solutions) that address the obstacles and constraints.

    E   **Evaluate** each of the solutions in light of the obstacles and constraints as they are weighted to determine a best possible solution.

    R   Develop and present a **Recommendation** with convincing support.

IDENTIFY AND CLARIFY THE PROBLEM, GATHERING AND ORGANIZING ALL RELEVANT INFORMATION.

4. Using the problem identified in step one, lead the class through each step of the POWER process. Thoroughly discuss the actions that occur in each step.

5. Upon completion, present a new situation. Have the students get into groups of three to four and develop a recommendation through the use of POWER. Have each group record its actions and reasoning throughout.

6. When the groups are finished, have each one report its recommendation, support, actions, and reasoning processes to the class.

7. Repeat this process over a period of time while increasing the complexity of the problems to be addressed.

Grade Level: Elementary, Middle, High School

Time: Varies

Special Materials: None

Motivational Standards: Enabling

Pluses: Block Schedules, Group Processing

QUICK TIP

4.48   QUICK ANTICIPATORY SETS

Often times we want a real fast way to actively engage and focus the students' minds. One way to accomplish this is to ask a question or pose a quick task that directly connects to the topic of the lesson. These quick tasks can be done either individually or by cooperative groups with sharing. The following are several examples, questions, and tasks that can be quite effective:

· Write three things you know about (the topic).

· What are the most important aspects of (the topic)?

· What pattern exists with (the topic)?

· What vehicle (car, train, boat, plane, ...) is most like (the topic), and why do you think so?

Thanks to Sue Tomaszewski for sharing this Quick Tip.

4.49   RECIPROCAL TEACHING

PURPOSE

To facilitate students gaining understanding from their reading.

DESCRIPTION

In many cases, students know how to read, but they don't possess effective strategies for developing meaning from what they are reading. This is a process that many successful readers either developed on their own or picked up along the way from their teachers.

Note: This process needs to be carefully modeled, taught, and practiced before groups of students are turned loose to follow the procedure explained below.

INSTRUCTIONAL USES

Instruction

TARGETED LEARNING

Reading, Conceptual Understanding, Information

PROCEDURE

1.   Have your students form reading groups - five is a good number.

2.   The students are to each *read* a short passage – no more than what they are to grasp in a single effort.

3. Have one student (the "summarizers") in each group *summarize* what was read. Other members of the group may add to the summary in an orderly, pre-determined manner. The teacher or a designated group leader may offer clues if the student summarizing is having difficulty.

4. The student summarizers then ask *information gathering questions* of their groups. The purpose of this step is to bring out specific information from the short passage that supports the summary. It is acceptable for the summarizer to refer back to the passage to help himself/herself formulate questions. The questions are to be answered based on what the group members can recall from their reading.

5. The summarizers then ask questions of their groups to help ensure *clarity/understanding*. Other members of the group may also ask questions to help them understand. An example question may sound something like, "I didn't quite understand the part about . . ., can someone explain what was meant?"

6. The summarizers ask the members of their groups to predict what will be in the next section to be read. The group should record the predictions.

7. Each group selects a new summarizer and the process continues.

Grade Level: Elementary, Middle, High School

Time: On-going

Special Materials: None

Motivational Standards: Involving, Successful, Enabling

Pluses: Block Schedules, Group Processing

Thanks to Kathy Gardner, former Assistant Superintendent for Tolleson Union High School District in Arizona, for introducing us to this strategy developed by Annemarie Palincsar and Anne Brown. Refer to "Reciprocal Teaching of Comprehension Fostering and Comprehension Monitoring Activities," *Cognition and Instruction* 1, 1984.

4.50 REFLECTION PAUSES

We once heard Dr. Kit Marshall refer to this as, "lingering over learning." After a point has been developed or learned, provide time for the students to reflect over the learning. Sometimes it is helpful to prompt the reflection with a specific prompt such as, "If you had known about this five years ago, how might your life be different today?" (Refer to the "Self-Assessment Prompts" in Chapter six.)

QUICK TIP

4.51   REFLECTION PROMPTS

PURPOSE

To promote meaningful reflection for self-evaluation and improvement.

DESCRIPTION

These prompts are designed to be used one at a time to encourage reflection. An excellent option for their use is to provide three prompts and ask the students to respond to the one that is most meaningful to them at the time.

INSTRUCTIONAL USES

Anticipatory Set, Closure, Transition

TARGETED LEARNING

Information, Skills

SAMPLE PROMPTS

1. What I did best today was …

2. I was excited to learn that …

3. The reason I'm learning this is …

4. What I liked best about what I learned was …

5. A question I have about what I'm learning is …

6. Some ways I might be able to use what I'm learning are …

7. If only people 500 years ago had known what I'm learning now, what probably would have happened differently is …

8. My thinking has changed from … to …

9. If I did this again, I would …

10. The best thing about my work is …

11. It is hard for me to learn … because …

12. If only … , it would be easier for me to learn …

13. I think what I'm learning is most like the color … because …

14. What I'm learning about is most like the animal … because …

15. What I'm learning is most like … because …

16. What I learned how to do today is …

17. I could best show what I've learned by …

18. If only …

19. If … knew this, …

20. Three things I could do even better are …

21. One thing I will do better is …

22. One way I will use what I've learned is …

23. One thing I can infer is … because …

24. One thing I can conclude … because …

25. I would predict that …

NOTE

Please refer to chapter six for additional prompts.

Grade Level: Elementary, Middle, High School

Time: 5-10 minutes

Special Materials: None

Motivational Standards: Enabling

Pluses: Block Schedules, Group Processing

4.52   ROUND ROBIN

PURPOSE

To check for learning while encouraging reflection and integration of the learning.

DESCRIPTION

Round Robin is a quick and easy strategy for eliciting feedback from students after a major concept has been taught. The entire activity takes approximately five minutes, yet it gives the teacher a quick snapshot of where the students are with the learning. It can be used any time during the class period when it is appropriate to check for learning.

INSTRUCTIONAL USES

Anticipatory Set, Closure, Transition

TARGETED LEARNING

Information, Skills, Perceptions

PROCEDURE

1. Ask the students to determine the one to three words that best capture what is most important or meaningful in the learning.

2. Ask each student to share his/her one to three words in turn.

3. Students may "pass" or piggyback on someone else's idea.

4. Respond only by saying "Thank you." (This strategy works best when the teacher doesn't give any verbal or non-verbal feedback that implies any value beyond valuing the fact that the student either gave a response or passed).

VARIATIONS

Ask students to share:

- applications;

- feelings about the concept; or

- a phrase or sentence that best summarizes the learning.

Grade Level: *Elementary, Middle, High School*

Time: *5 minutes*

Special Materials: *None*

Motivational Standards: *Involving, Caring*

Pluses: *Block Schedules, Group Processing*

Special thanks to Margaret McCabe and Jacqueline Rhoades for introducing us to this strategy.

4.53   SIMILES & METAPHORS

PURPOSE

To review and/or process information or concepts through a creative reasoning process.

DESCRIPTION

In the process of developing metaphors and similes, students find themselves recalling, analyzing, comparing, contrasting, interpreting, evaluating, and making connections, while learning a wonderful tool for enhancing communication. This is a fun way of addressing many of the reasoning skills while "swimming" in the content and increasing retention.

INSTRUCTIONAL USES

Anticipatory Set, Closure, Transition

TARGETED LEARNING

Information, Skills, Conceptual Understanding, Reasoning

PROCEDURE

1. Determine a rich and complex concept for the similes.

2. Tell the students they will be individually or collaboratively developing similes – give them several rich, insightful and fun examples.

3. Give the students the names of three common objects or animals as the basis for the simile. This works best if the students can see and touch pictures or models of the simile basis.

4. Have the students select one of the basis to use for their simile, and have them brainstorm as many of the important attributes of the concept as they can.

5. Give the students the concept(s), and have them brainstorm as many of the important attributes of the concept as they can.

6. Give the students two to three minutes to develop and write out their similes.

7. Have the students share their similes.

8. Show equal enthusiasm for each and every simile.

```
┌─────────────────────────────────┐
│            Similes              │
│  1.                             │
│    2.                           │
│      3.                         │
│  _____ is most like _____ │
│              because . . .      │
└─────────────────────────────────┘
```

VARIATION

Ask the students to name several common, complex objects to use as the simile bases.

Grade Level: Elementary, Middle, High School

Time: 10-15 minutes

Special Materials: None

Motivational Standards: Enabling

Pluses: Block Schedules, Group Processing, Multiple Intelligences

Similes

1.

2.

3.

_____ is most like _____ because . . .

4.54 SIMILE TRIADS

PURPOSE

To review, develop insights into, and/or process main points through metaphoric thinking.

DESCRIPTION

This strategy is excellent for introducing or drawing closure to a unit. Refer to the strategy *Similes & Metaphors* in this series for a shorter approach through metaphoric thinking.

INSTRUCTIONAL USES

Anticipatory Set, Closure, Transition

TARGETED LEARNING

Information, Skills, Conceptual Understanding, Reasoning

PROCEDURE

1. Determine the concepts to be processed.

2. Divide the class into groups of three to five each.

3. Draw a triangle like the one at the right on an overhead transparency, flip chart, or chalkboard, or pass out preprepared handouts.

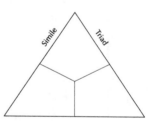

4. Ask each group's recorder to draw a similar triangle on a large sheet of butcher paper or on an overhead transparency (or handout).

5. Elicit from the whole class the names of three common objects. (Examples of common objects are radios, televisions, stoves, telephones, washers, and automobiles.) Have the group recorders write one in each section of the triangle.

6. Direct the groups to generate three to five similes for each common object and for the given concept. (Example: Equations are like automobiles because they take you where you need to go.)

7. Ask each group to select their favorite one to two similes to report to the whole class.

Grade Level: Elementary, Middle, High School

Time: 10-15 minutes

Special Materials: Chart paper, markers

Motivational Standards: Enabling

Pluses: Block Schedules, Group Processing, Multiple Intelligences

Special thanks to Robert Garmston for introducing us to this strategy.

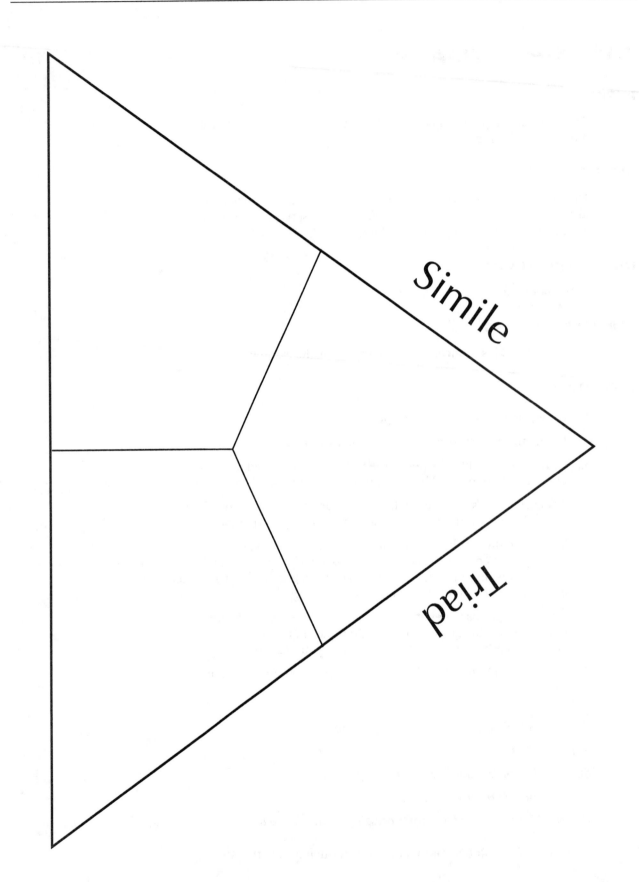

4.55   SKILL TEACHING

PURPOSE

To facilitate students' learning skills.

DESCRIPTION

Skill development requires the use of different approaches than concept development does. What follows is a number of techniques to add to your repertoire of teaching skills.

INSTRUCTIONAL USES

Instruction

TARGETED LEARNING

Skills

TECHNIQUES

1. Model performing the skill while thinking aloud for your students. Be certain to include all the important steps and decisions you have to make. It is helpful to record the steps, decisions, reminders, etcetera as you work your way through the skill for the students. The visual learners get to see you work through the skill, and the auditory learners get to concentrate on what you're saying and writing. To further help, you might draw little pictures where appropriate to help clarify what you are doing.

2. Provide students with flow charts for the skill/procedure. Teach them how to develop flow charts, and then have them develop their own for the skills you are teaching. This reinforces the skill for the students.

3. Provide for the students a set of written steps or procedures. Some students will like to have these as they watch you model. Others will want to focus on watching you, knowing they can refer to the written procedures when they are on their own.

4. If the skill is similar to others the students already know, provide them with analogies. Or perhaps even better, have them develop analogies or compare the new skill to skills they already possess.

5. Have the students use the new skill in contexts that require it. Strive to have these applications as authentic as possible. It is also beneficial if the applications are from outside the specific content area.

6. After the students have developed reasonable levels of proficiency and confidence with the skill, you can have them do an error analysis. Share with the students, and help them identify errors and mistakes to avoid when performing the skill. (See *Error Analysis*.)

7. Ask the students to locate and interview people outside of school who use the skill. Have them learn how the interviewee applies the skill and put together a presentation or a display to share with the class. (See *When Will I Ever Use This Stuff?*)

8. Deliberately plan for distributed practice with the new skill. During initial instruction, it is important to provide lots of concentrated practice. However, teach-practice-test is not adequate for long-term retention. Long-term retention requires that opportunities to practice the skill be provided over varying intervals until the end of the year. The time between practice opportunities should become greater and greater as the skill becomes internalized.

9. Direct your students to chart their progress in either accuracy, speed, complexity, or clarity with the skill. This is a means of providing the evidence of progress that is so essential for sustained motivation.

Grade Level: Elementary, Middle, High School

Time: Varies

Motivational Standards: Successful, Enabling

Pluses: Block Schedules, Group Processing

QUICK TIP

4.56 TEACH THE UNFAMILIAR THROUGH THE FAMILIAR

Whenever possible, teach concepts and skills by connecting/comparing them to those that are already known. Similes and metaphors help students learn faster and remember longer because they quickly provide meaning through connection to prior and outside knowledge.

4.57   TEAM HUDDLES

PURPOSE

To provide for group processing of information or questions. This strategy is a direct adaptation of Spencer Kagan's *Numbered Heads Together (Kagan 1990)*. It is an excellent strategy for engaging everyone in the class in the discussion of ideas or the answering of questions.

INSTRUCTIONAL USES

Anticipatory Set, Closure, Review, Instruction

TARGETED LEARNING

Information, Skills, Conceptual Understanding

PROCEDURE

1. Divide the class into mock football teams of four to five players each.

2. Give each team 30 seconds to select three possible team names for themselves. Tell the students their team names do NOT have to match real teams.

3. Go through each team, asking what name they would like while someone records the names on small cards. Each name can only be used once. Put the team cards in a pile to draw from randomly later.

4. Have each team assign roles/positions of quarterback, wide receiver, flanker, fullback, halfback. Only give them the number of positions that matches the smallest team in the class. Teams with the fewest players are to assign more than one position to some of their players until all the positions you are using are assigned.

5. Make sure you have a stack of position cards with a card for each position that you're using with the strategy.

6. Present the teams with a question to answer. The lower the level of the question the fewer consensus building skills the teams will need.

7. Have the teams HUDDLE to determine the response to the question on which they can all agree. Also, direct the teams to make sure that each team member can present their agreed upon response.

8. Blindly select a position card (or have a student select for you). Have all the students representing that position stand.

9. Blindly select a team card (or have a student select for you). At this point the standing person representing the selected position and team is to answer for his/her team. (Other standing team players may be encouraged to add to or refine.)

10. Have all sit down when it is agreed that a complete response has been provided.

11. This process can be continued as long as time and availability of meaningful questions permit.

Grade Level: *Elementary, Middle, High School*

Time: *30-45 minutes and up*

Special Materials: *Large index cards*

Motivational Standards: *Enabling*

Pluses: *Block Schedules, Group Processing*

QUICK TIP

4.58 THOUGHT PROVOKING QUESTIONS/PROMPTS

Focus on asking questions or prompting activities that stimulate thinking. The following are questions and prompts to help in this area:

- What might have happened if …?

- What could be the result of …?

- What conclusions can we draw from …

- How are these alike …?

- What might have happened if …?

- What could be the result of …?

- What conclusions can we draw from …

- How are these alike …?

- Construct/make/build/create/plan/design/fabricate …

- Compose/author …

- Analyze/infer/deduce/compare/contrast/equate

- Predict/conclude/infer/design/combine/integrate

- Solve (when there are multiple alternatives)

- evaluate/judge/critique

Refer to Chapter six for numerous other prompts and questions.

4.59   THREE QUESTIONS

PURPOSE

To facilitate reflection and conjecture.

DESCRIPTION

This activity is good for drawing closure at the end of a day or major lesson. It can be used as a "Door Pass" or a set of reflection prompts for a journal.

INSTRUCTIONAL USES

Closure, Transition

TARGETED LEARNING

Information

PROCEDURE

1. Have the students reflect for a few minutes over the following three prompts and then record their thoughts on a "Door Pass" (See *Door Pass* strategy) or in their journals:

    • What is one thing you feel validated in or that has been reinforced for you by this lesson?

    • What is one thing you learned?

    • What is one conjecture you have?

2. Remind the students to be clear and specific and not to just name topics.

HINT

Ask the students to be specific in their responses rather than just saying what they learned about. The older the student, the more likely he/she will play it safe and not provide an in-depth response. Be patient, provide many models, and persist.

VARIATION

Encourage students to respond by drawing a picture.

Grade Level: *Elementary, Middle, High School*

Time: *5-10 minutes*

Special Materials: *None*

Motivational Standards: *Enabling*

Pluses: *Block Schedules, Group Processing, Multiple Intelligences*

4.60 TIC TAC TOE

PURPOSE

To review concepts and skills.

DESCRIPTION

This strategy uses the age old game "Tic Tac Toe" to provide a fun twist for processing information.

INSTRUCTIONAL USES

Review, Instruction

TARGETED LEARNING

Information, Skills, Transition

PROCEDURE

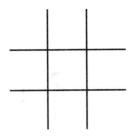

1. Write review problems or questions in the nine boxes of a tic tac toe board drawn in chalk on the board.

2. Cover the nine boxes with construction paper.

3. Have a member of the beginning team uncover a problem or question and attempt to complete it. If he/she does, then the question or problem is erased and the student places an X in that box.

4. Have a member of the other team choose a box and do the same. If he/she completes it correctly, the problem is erased and an O is placed in that box.

5. During this whole process, have the non-participating members of the two teams watch.

6. To keep them engaged and focused, tell them they may at any time say "stop" aloud if they notice an error.

7. If a team member does make an error, do not give the answer. The other team must work on the same problem or question.

8. Regular tic tac toe rules apply to win the game.

Note: The students love the anticipation of not knowing what is under each cover, plus the ability to stop an opponent and allow their own team a chance. This activity provides terrific review.

Grade Level: Elementary, Middle, High School

Time: 30 minutes

Special Materials: Chart paper, Construction paper

Motivational Standards: Enabling

Pluses: Block Schedules, Group Processing

4.61 TOTAL RECALL

PURPOSE

To provide for a complete reflection with respect to a previous lesson.

DESCRIPTION

Many review strategies are limited to surface recall. This strategy is designed to prompt in-depth reflection.

INSTRUCTIONAL USES

Anticipatory Set, Closure, Review, Transition

TARGETED LEARNING

Information

PROCEDURE

1. Provide each student with a full size sheet of paper with a triangle similar to the example included with this strategy.

2. Explain to the students what is meant by each of the terms in the triangle and give them examples for each.

3. Ask the students to individually reflect over the previous class period, lesson, or unit and identify significant recollections, observations, feelings, and insights. Have them briefly record them on their triangle.

4. Put the students into groups of four to five and have them share what they've recorded. Have each student record on his/her triangle the reflections of the others.

   • Have the students share their important learnings and use their questions as "frames" for the next assignment. They need to be searching for the answers as they continue to study and work with the material.

- Have the students turn in their thoughts and questions to you. This information can be very useful in regards to what the students really learned and where they still have questions. These questions become great "frames" for future lessons.

VARIATIONS

This strategy works very well when done orally in small groups of 2-3 students.

Grade Level: Elementary, Middle, High School

Time: 10 minutes

Special Materials: Paper with triangle printed on it

Motivational Standards: Enabling

Pluses: Block Schedules, Group Processing, Multiple Intelligences

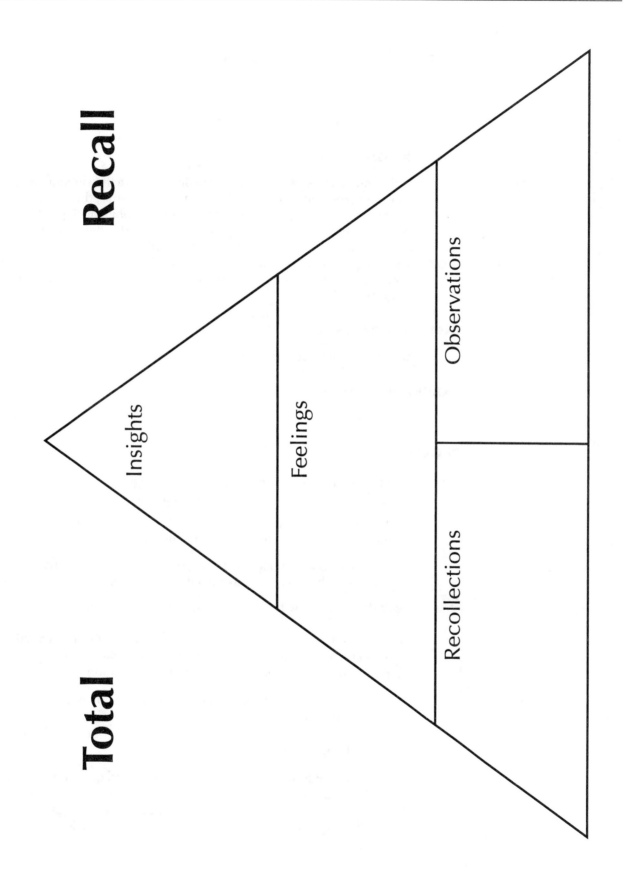

4.62   TWO STARS & A WISH

PURPOSE

To draw closure or provide an anticipatory set.

DESCRIPTION

At the end of a lesson it is always beneficial to have the students spend a few moments reflecting over the learning. Of course, this is also helpful before we begin a lesson that builds on prior learning. The problem is that students often have trouble with this because they do not know how to focus on the most important ideas. This strategy is designed to help the learners narrow their thinking. It can be used with any age level and any content. The time necessary for the strategy is also very flexible.

INSTRUCTIONAL USES

Anticipatory Set, Closure, Transition

TARGETED LEARNING

Information

PROCEDURE

1. At the end of a lesson or a unit, or before beginning a unit, have the students take out their journals or notebooks.

2. Ask students to identify the two thoughts or concepts they think are most important and to explain why they think so.

3. Ask students to also identify the one thought or concept about which they have a question or need clarification.

4. At this point there are several things that can be done:

    • Have the students share their thoughts and questions with the class or a smaller group. Allow time for students to compare major ideas and to answer each other's questions.

    • Have the students share their important learnings and use their questions as "frames" for the next assignment. They need to be searching for the answers as they continue to study and work with the material.

    • Have the students turn in their thoughts and questions to you. This information can be very useful in regards to what the students really learned and where they still have questions. These questions become great "frames" for future lessons.

VARIATION

This strategy works very well when done orally in small groups of two to three students.

> *Grade Level:* Elementary, Middle, High School
>
> *Time:* 5-10 minutes
>
> *Special Materials:* None
>
> *Motivational Standards:* Enabling, Valuable
>
> *Pluses:* Block Schedules, Group Processing, Multiple Intelligences

Special thanks to Dr. Kit Marshall for introducing us to this strategy.

4.63 VENN DIAGRAMS FOR BUILDING KNOWLEDGE

PURPOSE

To promote the development and refinement of students' knowledge.

DESCRIPTION

One of the ways in which students can develop their knowledge of something is through comparison. In this strategy, the students are asked to use a Venn Diagram in order to enhance their knowledge by comparing two concepts, topics, or procedures. (Examples: linear and quadratic solution procedures or applications, characters in two novels, causes for two wars, solutions for two complex problems in science or math.)

Note: the following procedure needs to be carefully modeled, taught, and practiced outside of the content area before it is used to enhance the learning of content concepts or skills.

INSTRUCTIONAL USES

Instruction

TARGETED LEARNING

Information, Conceptual Understanding, Skills

PROCEDURE

1. Provide your students with "two-circle Venn diagrams" or have them draw their own. Have them label the two circles with the two "things" being compared. (One thing on one circle, and the other thing on the other circle.)

2. With the class, develop the list of characteristics or attributes that will be compared. (For example, if they are to compare apples and oranges, the list of characteristics may include shape, taste, uses, season, history, place of origin, myths about, etcetera.)

3. For each characteristic or attribute in the list, have the students put the corresponding description/information in the appropriate location on the Venn diagram:

    *   true for only the orange - in that portion of the orange's circle that is not overlapped by the apple's circle;

    *   true for only the apple - in that portion of the apple's circle that is not overlapped by the orange's circle;

    *   true for both the apple and the orange - in that part of the Venn diagram where the two circles overlap

4. Ask the students to develop summaries that convey the commonalties and differences. You might also want to ask them to develop a conclusion based on their analysis.

Grade Level: Elementary, Middle, High School

Time: Varies

Special Materials: Venn Diagram Handouts

Motivational Standards: Involving, Enabling

Pluses: Block Schedules, Group Processing

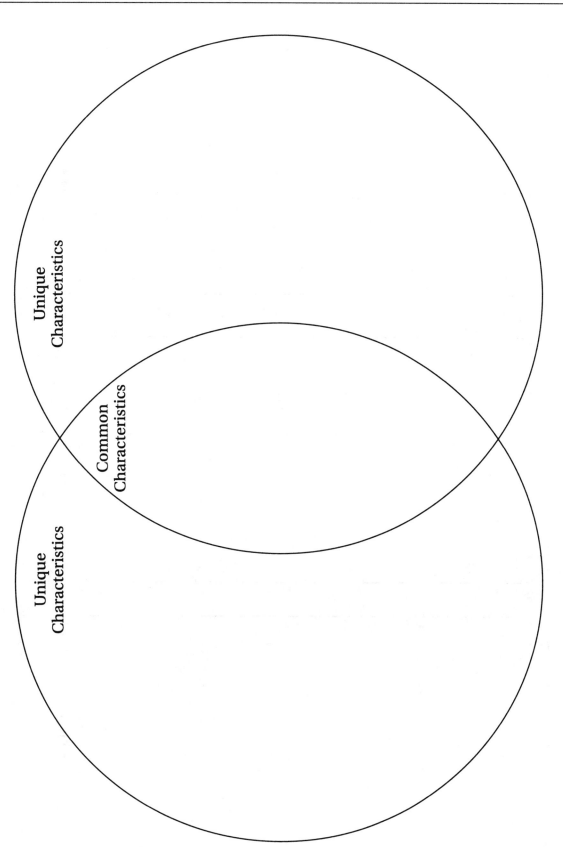

4.64 WALKABOUT

PURPOSE

To provide for a quick review after one or more days of instruction.

DESCRIPTION

During this strategy the students "walk about" the room gathering recollections of the previous lessons from one another. They take with them a map on a full size sheet of paper.

INSTRUCTIONAL USES

Anticipatory Set, Closure, Review, Instruction, Transition

TARGETED LEARNING

Information, Skills, Conceptual Understanding

PROCEDURE

1. Give each student a copy of a blank map of Australia divided into six regions (representing the six states and territories of Australia). Each state or territory is labeled appropriately.

2. Before the "walkabout," provide enough time for each student to refresh his/her memory by writing on the back of his/her map as many things as he/she can remember from previous lessons.

3. Then give the students time to "walk about" the room filling their maps with different recollections from other students. (nine minutes is usually about right.) Ask the students to get only one recollection from each of the other students and record at least one recollection in each state or territory. Each person should sign his/her name in the space where his/her recollection has been written.

Grade Level: *Elementary, Middle, High School*

Time: *10-40 minutes (varies based on scope of material)*

Special Materials: *Copy of Australian map or another map. Limit the map sections to six.*

Motivational Standards: *Enabling*

Pluses: *Block Schedules, Group Processing, Multiple Intelligences*

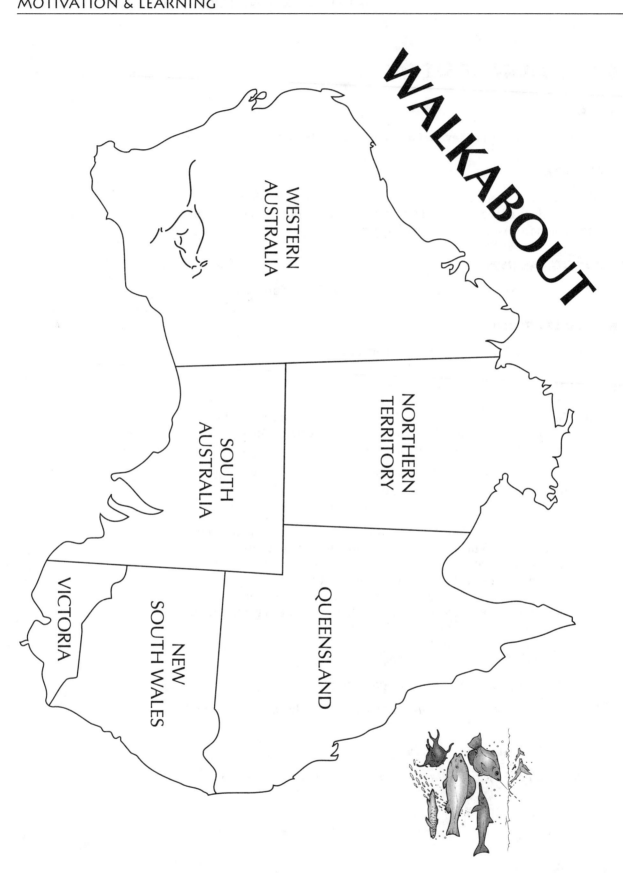

WALKABOUT

4.65 "WHAT IF?" CHALLENGES

PURPOSE

To provide for review, higher level thinking, and/or to provide for lively discussions about the subject matter.

DESCRIPTION

This is a strategy for putting a little fun into processing information or review.

INSTRUCTIONAL USES

Anticipatory Set, Instruction

TARGETED LEARNING

Conceptual Understanding, Reasoning

PROCEDURE

1. Develop a "What If" question such as, "What if Columbus had discovered California instead of a Caribbean island?" Be certain the question is relevant to your curriculum.

2. Develop about five different conjectures with logical, factually supported justifications.

3. Divide the class into teams of two to four students each. Be certain that team roles are identified. Also be certain that the teams are such that there is no feeling of being labeled.

4. Ask the teams to develop as many conjectures as they can with an accurate, logical supporting statement for each. Provide them with enough time to match the amount of depth, creativity, and in or out of class supporting research that you want.

5. Challenge the class by saying something like, "Let's see how many teams can come up with at least two conjectures that I have."

6. Have the teams present their conjectures and justifications to the class. Have the statements of conjecture and defense put on sheets of paper.

7. Have the students tape their conjectures to the wall. Have them separate them into groups based on similarities.

8. Present your conjectures and put them in the appropriate groups on the wall.

9. Ask how many teams developed conjectures similar to at least one of yours.

Grade Level: Elementary, Middle, High School

Time: 30 minutes

Special Materials: Notebook paper

Motivational Standards: Enabling

Pluses: Block Schedules, Group Processing

4.66 WHAT? WHY? & HOW?

PURPOSE

To facilitate learning of a transferable process.

DESCRIPTION

This activity is particularly valuable when we would like the students to begin learning a process that they can adapt and use elsewhere. It is also valuable when you suspect that some students may not see the value in what was done and you wish to maintain a positive atmosphere by having students provide positive reasons for doing what was done.

In addition, one of the common characteristics of very successful people is that they have learned to study what other very successful people do so that they can modify and use the procedures in their own situations. This strategy helps to reinforce this characteristic.

INSTRUCTIONAL USES

Transition, Closure, Reflection, Skills

TARGETED LEARNING

Skills

PROCEDURE

1. After you and the students have worked through an activity like many in this series, have the students individually reflect over what has transpired and respond to the following three questions in their learning logs:

    • By doing what we just did, **What** did we accomplish?

    • **Why** did we do what we did?

    • **How** might you be able to use what we did?

2. Either in groups or as a whole class, debrief the reflection.

HINT

This same strategy can be used by working through the same questions with respect to something someone else has done.

Grade Level: Elementary, Middle, High School

Time: 10 minutes

Special Materials: None

Motivational Standards: Enabling

Pluses: Block Schedules, Group Processing

4.67   WHO OR WHAT AM I?

PURPOSE

To provide an active review or introduction to a topic.

DESCRIPTION

This activity is a fun, safe, interactive way to engage students in reviewing information or bringing prior learning forward. The basic format is a take-off on a TV show called, "What's My Line?"

INSTRUCTIONAL USES

Anticipatory Set, Closure, Review, Ice Breaker

TARGETED LEARNING

Information

PROCEDURE

1. Post a list of the important topics, concepts, events, or people.

2. Make up at least one 3 x 5 card for each student in the class by putting one of the items from step one on each card. The items may be repeated.

3. Go over the list with the students, and make sure the list is such that the students can see it from anywhere in the classroom.

4. Show the cards to the students. Tell them they will all have one of the cards taped to their backs.

5. Have students form small groups and let them see the cards on each

other's backs. They are not to tell one another what's on each other's backs. Students ask questions of one another until they can say to their group, "I think I'm (an item from Step one) because (this) is what I know." They keep playing until they "get it."

6.   They may switch groups if they wish.

HINT

Play for 5-15 minutes – be careful not to drag it out too long. Switch people and keep putting new cards on people, so that when time is finally called, most, if not all students are engaged in playing.

Grade Level: *Elementary, Middle, High School*

Time: *5-10 minutes*

Special Materials: *3 x 5 cards, Tape*

Motivational Standards: *Valuable*

Pluses: *Block Schedules, Group Processing, Multiple Intelligences*

4.68   WRITING CLEAR DIRECTIONS

PURPOSE

To teach students how to develop effective written or oral directions for processes.

DESCRIPTION

This is a fun and lively strategy that helps students learn how to write more effective directions and procedures. The students write directions for putting on a T-shirt. The directions are to be written so they are effective with anyone who will follow them literally.

INSTRUCTIONAL USES

Instruction

TARGETED LEARNING

Skills

PROCEDURE

1. Divide the class into groups of two or three.

2. Ask them how many times they've been frustrated because they couldn't seem to follow directions written by someone else and get the results they wanted. Have them talk about their experiences.

3. Tell them they will be learning how to write a set of QUALITY directions.

4. Hold up a common T-shirt. Make sure it has a picture on either the front or the back, but not both.

5. Tell the teams they will have 10 minutes to develop and write a set of directions for putting on the T-shirt.

6. Advise them they are to assume that anyone reading the directions will not have their knowledge, and will consequently do EXACTLY what the directions say.

7. Tell them at the end of the 10 minutes an impartial reader will be selected to read the directions which you will follow exactly.

8. At the end of 10 minutes, ask groups to volunteer to have their directions tested. Select a reader from another group to read the directions EXACTLY as they are written.

9. As the directions are read, do exactly what is said, while getting away with any mistake that the directions will allow. For example, if the directions say to put your arms in the arm holes, put the wrong arms in the wrong arm holes, or put your arms in the correct arm holes – but from the outside in rather than from the inside out.

10. Make sure that the blame is on you for being so "block-headed."

11. After two to three sets of directions have failed, give them back to the groups for adjustments and try again.

12. After the students get the idea, begin having them describe how to do subject matter procedures that they already have learned well in previous years. After they become good at that, move to using oral and written descriptions of procedures in your regular teaching and assessment practices.

Special thanks to Barbara Benson of Boone, North Carolina for introducing us to this strategy.

VARIATIONS

This can be done with procedures for putting on a jacket that buttons, making a peanut butter and jelly sandwich, or putting together a simple object with Tinker Toys.

HINT

If you are going to pick your own procedures to work with, make sure the task isn't too complicated. Something like tying shoes sounds easy, but writing directions for it is far more complex than most people realize.

Grade Level: Elementary, Middle, High School

Time: 30 minutes

Special Materials: T-shirt

Motivational Standards: Valuable, Enabling, Involving

Pluses: Block Schedules, Group Processing, Multiple Intelligences

4.69 X-FILE

PURPOSE

To develop a greater understanding of complex concepts.

DESCRIPTION

This strategy works best as a "challenge game." The object of the game is for a group of students to get the members of the class to name a concept. The group does this by giving any hints they choose – but they may not use any restricted words that are listed in their "X-FILE." This strategy is fun for the students while at the same time creating a learning situation in which they must have a solid understanding of the concept and be creative in the hints they give.

INSTRUCTIONAL USES

Review

TARGETED LEARNING

Information, Conceptual Understanding, Reasoning

PROCEDURE

1. Determine the concept(s) or skill(s) that you wish the students to describe.

2. Develop lists of associated keywords for each concept that the students are NOT to use in their descriptions, and put the lists in what will be the groups' "X-FILES."

3. Give the class the directions and information they will need.

   - Each group will be given two minutes to prepare for their turn.
   - Each group will have three minutes to give any school appropriate hints they choose until the members of the class can identify the group's concept.
   - Groups are not to say any of the "keywords" listed in their "X-FILES."
   - If a group forgets and uses one of the restricted keywords, they must pass their turn.

4. The activity tends to be enough fun through its challenge and novelty – do not assign points, competitive elements, or other extrinsic motivators.

   Example 1:   X-FILE Concept = iambic pentameter

   Key-Words that are restricted = poetry, meter, Shakespeare

   Example 2:   X-FILE Concept = rain

   Key-Words that are restricted = clouds, sky, water

HINTS

This strategy works best toward the end of a major unit, semester, or year. It is important to have enough concepts on which to draw for the game to be challenging and fun. This strategy tends to be easiest for people who are strong in linguistic and mathematical intelligences. Take the time to support and coach so the activity stays fun, safe, and challenging for all.

Grade Level: Elementary, Middle, High School

Time: 30 minutes

Special Materials: List of "key words"

Motivational Standards: Involving, Valuable

Pluses: Block Schedules, Group Processing, Multiple Intelligences

4.70   YOU CAN HAVE ...
BUT YOU CAN'T HAVE ...

PURPOSE

To provide a quick review before beginning a lesson.

DESCRIPTION

This activity requires students to think about a concept by identifying "things" that fit the concept and "things" that don't fit it. When first introducing this activity, it is best to name the specific concept with which the students are working.

INSTRUCTIONAL USES

Anticipatory Set, Closure, Review, Transition

TARGETED LEARNING

Information, Conceptual Understanding

PROCEDURE

1. The teacher begins the activity by giving something that fits and something that doesn't the concept, then asking the students to add to the list.

    Note: As the students get older and more skilled in the type of thinking this activity requires, it provides great practice for the type of thinking required when working with analogies, similes, and metaphors.

    Example: Eastern States is the concept.

    "You can have New York, but you can't have California."

    "You can have New Hampshire, but you can't have Nevada."

2. Once the students are familiar with the strategy, try it without first giving the concept with which they are working. Again, this requires more complex thinking on the part of the students.

    Examples:

    "You can have Piccaso, but you can't have Hemmingway."

    "You can have Rembrandt, but you can't have Shakespeare."

    (The concept is artist as opposed to authors.)

"You can have lions, but you can't have sheep."

"You can have elephants, but you can't have horses."

(The concept is jungle wildlife.)

VARIATIONS:

Looks like . . . doesn't look like.

Is . . . is not.

Grade Level: *Elementary, Middle, High School*

Time: *5 minutes*

Special Materials: *None*

Motivational Standards: *Enabling*

Pluses: *Block Schedules, Group Processing*

CHAPTER 5

COLLABORATIVE

GROUPS

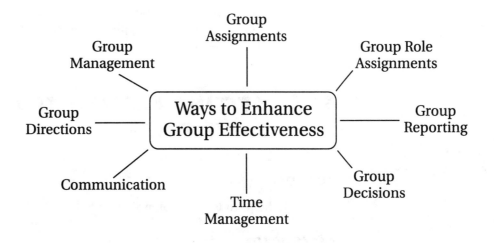

QUICK TIP

5.1 BRAINSTORMING – 5 QUICK TIPS

1. Break into brainstorm groups of five students each. Groups with fewer than five or more than six tend not to generate as many options.

2. Set and adhere to an established time limit (typically three to five minutes).

3. Make certain before starting, that everyone understands that judgment and discussion are to be deferred until later. Have a designated referee that throws a towel or something else soft into the air whenever . . .

   • an evaluative comment is made,

   • non-verbal judgments are made, or

   • discussion of an idea begins.

4. Before accepting ideas for the brainstorm list, have each person write down as many ideas as he/she can (brain-writing).

5. Before starting, encourage humor to surface, and keep it fun as the session progresses. People tend to generate more ideas when they're having fun.

5.2 GETTING ACQUAINTED ADVENTURE

PURPOSE

To help students become acquainted and feel comfortable in a group.

DESCRIPTION

People tend to feel more comfortable when they know they have a lot in common with the others in their group. In this activity the students use Venn diagrams to find things they have in common with one another.

USES

Group Effectiveness

PROCEDURE

1. Have the students form groups of three or assign groups of three. Be certain students are protected from exclusion.

2. Provide each group with a sheet of paper that has a Venn diagram with three circles and that fills the page.

3. Ask the students to label the circles – one for each student in the group.

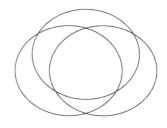

4. Have the students individually write as many things as they can about themselves that they think the others in their group may have in common with them. Tell them they will have two minutes to write as many things as they can think of. Encourage them to organize their ideas. Give them some examples to consider such as:

   • having a pet

   • enjoying volleyball

   • favorite television programs, sports, or hobbies

   • favorite movies

   • chores

5. Give the groups three minutes to share as many characteristics as they can and to determine their common characteristics. Do this by asking the students to take turns sharing one characteristic at a time. With each characteristic shared – the group "leader" checks which other group members have the same item and then puts it in the Venn diagram appropriately. You may want to challenge them to see which groups have:

   • the most in common, and

   • the most number of characteristics charted.

6. Have each group announce what they found they have in common. Keep a running tally on the board or overhead. With each common characteristic, poll the other groups to see how many also came up with it.

Grade Level: *Elementary, Middle, High School*

Time: *Varies*

Special Materials: *Venn Diagram, paper and pencils*

Motivational Standards: *Involving, Valuable*

Pluses: *Block Schedules, Group Processing*

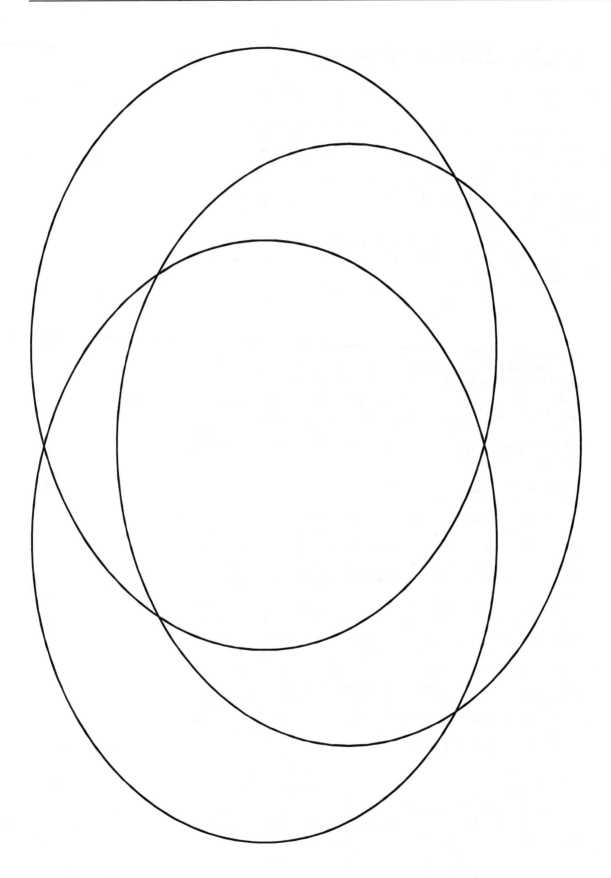

5.3   GROUP DECISIONS

PURPOSE

To facilitate a group converging to a decision from many options.

DESCRIPTION

Often times a group is faced with many options and just as many opinions. When the options need to be narrowed to just a few or one, too often, the result is anger and hurt feelings.

Robert Garmston and Bruce Wellman in their "Premiere Facilitation" workshops teach a process for avoiding, or at least reducing, conflicts during these difficult situation.

USES

Group Effectiveness

PROCEDURE

1. Post the options that are to be reduced in number on chart paper. Be careful to list the options in as random an order as you can.

2. Label each of the options as best you can to avoid placing value or worth. Letters (A,B, C) tend to be better than numbers (1, 2, 3).

3. Provide a period for clarification of each of the options. During this period, any student can ask to have an option clarified. The person who suggested the option, or is most knowledgeable about the option in question is to provide the clarification. This is for clarification only – not defending or arguing for the option. After an option has been clarified, check to be certain the clarification was adequate. Allow time for all the options to be clarified as need be.

4. Provide a period of time for advocacy. During this period, students are asked to make specific supportive statements about any and all of the options. If they can think of any positive statement about any of the options, they are to make it. Encourage the students to listen carefully and build almost a synergy of positive observations. Enforce advocacy. No comparisons can be made, and no negative points can be stated. Allow this to continue until no one can think of any additional positive comments. It is sometimes helpful if you chime in when a lull develops with an advocacy statement that opens a new direction of thought.

5. As a group, reduce the number of options by about one-third. To do this, determine the number that is about two-thirds the total number of options. For an example, let's assume there are a total of twelve options. Two-thirds of twelve is eight. In this example, we would reduce the number of options to eight. Ask each student to

select the eight options that he/she thinks are best based on all that they've heard. (For the remaining steps in this procedure, we will continue to use these example numbers.)

6. One by one, for each option, take a tally of the number of students that selected it as one of their eight best options.

7. From the twelve original options, select the eight that have been selected by the most number of students as one of the eight best.

8. If eight options are too many for your purposes, continue from here with another round of advocacy statements, selecting the best two-thirds (go for five or six based on group preference).

9. Continue the process until the group has worked its way down to the ideal number of options for the given situation.

HINT

There will be tremendous temptation to circumvent the process. Don't! Allowing negative statements or comparisons will result in anger or withdrawal on the part of some students. Eliminating too many options in any one pass will result in students not having at least one of their selections in the next round.

Grade Level: Elementary, Middle, High School

Time: Varies

Motivational Standards: Involving, Safe

Pluses: Block Schedules

QUICK TIP

5.4 GROUP DIRECTIONS

Whenever you are giving directions to a group, it is helpful to remember that you have students with many different styles and perspectives. Many students are not strong auditory learners and perform better if they can see the directions for a given task. Take the time to develop and reproduce or display on an overhead, your directions—particularly if there are more than three steps involved. **Also, test your directions with one or two colleagues to be certain they work well for others.**

5.5 GROUP REPORTING

When you are using cooperative strategies and there are more than six groups to report, the reporting can take too long. This causes the class to become bored and lose energy. Before the groups begin reporting, inform the class that only four to six groups will be reporting – the number should be determined by the complexity, diversity, and lengthiness of the reports. It is important to make sure that all groups get opportunities to report from time to time.

QUICK TIP

5.6 GROUP TIME NEGOTIATION

PURPOSE

To keep timelines tight for group activities while using group involvement in establishing timelines.

DESCRIPTION

As all of us who have given groups too much time know, it is much better to provide groups with too little time and adjust as needed than to have idle time. However, if we always have to provide extra time, students quickly learn they don't need to work as quickly as you might like. The following is a procedure we can follow to be certain timelines are tight and everyone knows they need to be efficient and timely.

USES

Group Management

PROCEDURE

1. Determine how long the group task should take if everyone stays on task and focused.

2. If the students have enough knowledge of the group task to be done, give the groups 30 seconds to decide what they think is an appropriate amount of time. If the estimates aren't even in the ballpark, facilitate a discussion to help the students gain a clearer picture of what's expected.

3. If the estimates are in the ballpark, pick a time that is closest to the shortest and say something like, "Since some of you think it can be done in "x" minutes, and some think even less, let's set "x" minutes as the time. I'll monitor your progress as you're working. Please begin now."

4. If the students actually need more time when the time is up, repeat the process with a slight variation. First, give the groups that need more time 20 seconds to decide how much time they need. Then poll the groups and give them the amount of time you think they need and is within the time limits given by the students.

5. Before you ask them to begin again, tell the students what they should do if their group finishes before the time is up.

6. When the time is up, be certain you have a meaningful, value added discussion planned that will allow a group that needs more time to finish quickly.

Grade Level: Elementary, Middle, High School

Time: 3 minutes

Special Materials: Timer or stopwatch

Motivational Standards: Caring, Involving

Pluses: Block Schedules, Group Processing

QUICK TIP

5.7 GROUP ROLES - 20 QUICK TIPS

The following are offered as ways to select members of groups for different roles such as time keeper, process keeper, reporter, recorder, and materials officer.

It is important that the roles the students serve in during group activities be rotated regularly. Always look for ways that this can happen.

HINT

These tips have been found to be fun and generally non-threatening in role assignments. However, it is essential to assess and respect the needs and sensitivities of all the students in the classroom.

20 WAYS TO MAKE ROLE ASSIGNMENTS

For the role of _____ , it will be the person . . .

1. with the longest/shortest hair

2. your group selects who is willing to perform in the role

3. with the darkest/lightest hair

4. with the most/least buttons

5. with the most/least/largest/smallest pockets

6. wearing the most/least "dressy" outfit

7. whose birthday is closest to today or farthest from today

8. whose phone number gives the greatest total when you add all the digits

9. with the most/least number of letters in both his/her first and last names

10. whose birthday is closest to January 1st

11. with the smallest/biggest shoes

12. who has the greatest/least phone number as an actual number

13. who hasn't served in the role for the longest time

14. wearing the brightest colors

15. wearing the most of any particular color

16. with the darkest/lightest eyes

17. with the prettiest elbow/thumb/pinkie

18. wearing the fewest/most colors

19. members volunteer

20. Perhaps our favorite way of selecting an unpopular role like reporter is one we call SELECT & SWITCH. This method works best in groups of five or more people. Have the students get ready to point to the person in their group that they want to be the reporter. Tell them not to point until you give the signal. When ready, have the students point to their selected group member. After the laughter dies down, have the person who received the most "points" identify him/herself. When all can hear clearly, announce that the person who has just been selected is now to select the reporter for the group. After all the laughter, be sure to have each group tell you who its reporter is.

QUICK TIP

5.8   GROUP TIMELINES

When first working with a group of students, it is important to keep timelines tight and to make expectations concerning timeliness very clear.

This is best accomplished through actions rather than through words; however, it is also important to remember that these actions must be gentle, supportive, and consistent. Therefore, when first involving students in timed activities, pay close attention to the following:

- set the allotted time so that most students will be rushed;

- be certain that at the end of the allotted time, you are completely ready to begin the next phase or activity. Also, be certain that you have placed yourself at your appropriate teaching position (See "Teaching Positions"); and

- be certain to monitor the students' progress so that you may negotiate time extensions as necessary. (See "Group Time Negotiation.")

QUICK TIP

5.9   GROUP TIME MAINTENANCE

Use a three step signal when timing cooperative group activities.

1. Tell the students how long they will have to complete the task and that you will give them a 30 second warning.

2. When there are 30 seconds remaining, announce, "30 more seconds – please finish what you are doing."

3. At precisely 30 seconds or when there is a lull in talking, whichever comes first, say, "Thank you." Then begin immediately with whatever is next.

5.10 GROUPING BY APPOINTMENT

PURPOSE

To group students and build a collaborative classroom.

DESCRIPTION

Having the opportunity to work and dialogue with people is a very important part of learning and successful functioning in an interpersonal work or social environment. "Real-life" context is simulated when students make appointments with each other in order to collaborate and share ideas.

USES

Group Assignments

PROCEDURE

1. Give each student an Appointment Calendar that shows one week - Sunday through Saturday.

2. Have each student set up an appointment for each day of the week with a different classmate. This is normally done by having all the students move around the room at one time. It is very important to remind the students that they each need to sign each other's calendars!

3. Help students by asking (after a few minutes) who still needs appointments and get these students together.

4. When it is appropriate to pair students, announce a day of the week and have the students meet with their scheduled appointment for that day.

HINT

Having the students do their Appointment Calendars on Monday for the entire week is a good way to manage this strategy.

VARIATION

Follow the same procedure as above, substituting an Appointment Clock for the Calendar. This strategy allows for numerous appointments and is good to use when the learning is supported by many opportunities for varied discussions and/or feedback. Typically, appointments are set for 3:00, 6:00, 9:00, and 12:00 only.

Grade Level: *Elementary, Midd!le, High School*

Time: *5 minutes*

Special Materials: *Appointment calendars or clocks*

Motivational Standards: *Valuable*

Pluses: *Block Schedules, Multiple Intelligences*

Thanks to Dr. Kit Marshall for introducing us to this strategy.

Appointment Calendar

Monday	
Tuesday	
Wednesday	
Thursday	
Friday	

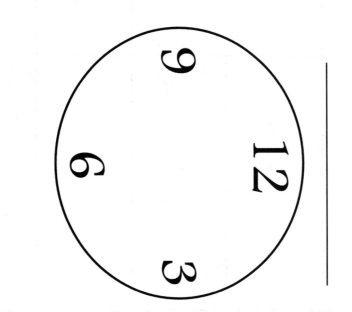

Appointment Clock

5.11 GROUPING BY DECADE

This grouping strategy is appropriate for adult groups. We have included it because it's so much fun.

Ask the students (participants in a workshop) to line up based on the decade of their high school graduation. (We suggest you divide the 60's into two groups, those who graduated before 1965 and those who graduated from 1965 through 1969.)

Have the people in each group share the major events/situations they remember from their graduation decade. Ask each group to share two major events with the whole class (workshop).

Ask each group to determine and share with the whole group how the major events of their decade affected them.

QUICK TIP

5.12 GROUPING BY SILENT BIRTHDAY LINE-UPS

PURPOSE

To put students into random groups in a fun and exciting way.

DESCRIPTION

In this strategy, the students are asked to line up by birthday without talking.

USES

Group Assignment

PROCEDURE

1. Explain to the students that their task is to form a single line according to when they were born. The line is to begin with those students who were born on or close to January 1st and end with those born on or close to December 31st. Tell students that no oral or written communication is allowed. Any other form of communication is acceptable and encouraged. Tell them to be creative.

2. Ask students to line up in order according to their birthdays.

3. Once the line is complete, have students standing close to each other talk to verify birth dates and make any necessary adjustments.

4. Then, divide students into groups or pairs. Several suggestions for grouping are as follows:

    • students count off 1 through 4 and become a 4 person team;

    • fold the line - have the ends of each line come to the middle and count off the number necessary to form teams; or

    • find the middle of the line and divide the line into two parts. Then have the two lines come together and form groups of four. (This looks like a Wedding Procession).

EXTENSION

Use this strategy to introduce the concept of probability. (Example: What are the chances of two students having the same birthday?)

Grade Level: Elementary, Middle, High School

Time: 5 minutes

Motivational Standards: Valuable

Pluses: Block Schedules, Multiple Intelligences

QUICK TIP

5.13   GROUP ASSIGNMENTS: A BAKER'S DOZEN OF QUICK TIPS

Several of the grouping strategies represented here involve asking students to use much of their own initiative. Whenever this occurs, it involves a certain amount of risk. In such activities, monitor carefully, being sure to watch for those who may need help and guidance in finding a group or partner. Also, you might want to designate a place in the classroom where people who have not yet found a group can congregate. Be sure to help quickly and unobtrusively those that congregate in this safe area.

1.   COLORED CARDS

Randomly pass out cards that are assorted colors, or have colored marks on them, but be certain you have planned the number of colors to work right. Ask the students to form groups of x number of people with:

> • the same color cards

> • different color cards

2.   COLORED MARKERS

Arrange the tables or desks into the size groups you desire. Put a different set of colored marker pens at each group location, being certain that all the pens at any location are all the same color. Ask the students as they come in to sit with whomever they choose. As soon as the students are all in their seats, ask them to produce something such as name cards using the marker pens at their locations. Then, ask the students to form new groups consisting of members who used different colored pens for their products.

Variation: Put marker pens at each group location, being certain that there are enough pens for each student to use his/her own and that all the pens at each location are different colors. Then ask the students to form new groups consisting of members who used the same colored pens to create their products.

3.   PLAYING CARDS

Pass out the cards from a deck of playing cards, being certain that you have pre-selected the cards that will result in the groups you desire. Ask the students to form groups of x number of people with:

- different suits
- same suits
- same card values
- different card values

4.   HANDS HIGH

Ask the students to each raise one hand high. Tell them to keep their hands up until they have found other people to form a group of x number of people. Tell them they can lower their hands when they have formed a complete group and are ready to sit down. (This grouping strategy is designed to create totally voluntary grouping.)

5.   PERSONAL COLORS

Ask the students to form groups of x number of people with either the same or different colors. Be ready to help people bend the rules a little to get the last groups filled. Ideas for colors are:

- houses
- shoes
- hair
- eyes
- articles of clothing
- primary family car
- favorite color (have them write this down ahead of time)

6. MULTIPLE INTELLIGENCES

Administer a multiple intelligence assessment to help the students identify what may be their greater intelligences. Then have the students form groups of *x* number of people of either similar strengths or different strengths. (Caution – Do not place value on any intelligence over any other or in any way attempt to rank within the different intelligences.)

7. FOUR CORNERS

Identify four items or concepts. Label the four corners of the room with items or concepts you've identified. Have each of the students decide which of the four things he/she most relates to and move to the corresponding corner. Examples of what the corners can be labeled can come from the following:

- favorite sports
- favorite foods
- types of plants
- types of animals
- geometric shapes

- types of music
- talents or skills
- scientific principles
- great people in history or literature

After the students move to the corner that represents their choice, provide time for them to discuss why they made the choice they did.

Once the students are in their selected corners, have them break into groups of whatever size you desire.

8. BACKGROUND KNOWLEDGE

Sometimes it is advantageous to have students grouped so that they represent similar or different strengths in their backgrounds. Either provide a clear and precise rubric that the students can use to determine the strengths of their backgrounds or use your expertise to identify the background strengths of the students. Then either divide them into groups of *x* number of people of similar or different background knowledge or ask them to do it themselves.

9. CHARACTERISTIC LINE-UPS

Have the students line up based on a characteristic such as length of hair. Then starting at one end of the line, you can break off groups of whatever size you desire. Another option is to fold the line by having the students come together from each end of the line to form groups. Characteristics around which you can have students line up include:

- length of hair

- alphabetically by the name of favorite foods, restaurants, or anything else

- height

- length of arm (including finger nails)

- numerical order by street address or P.O. Box #

- shoe size

- important date in their lives

- month and day of their birthdays

10. COMIC STRIPS

Cut out numerous comic strips and cut apart the panels. The more the comic strip is relevant to the topic the better. Give each student a panel. Then ask the students to search the room to find the others that it takes to complete the comic strip. Variations on this idea include using cut up pieces of pictures, single panel cartoons, cut up reproductions of famous paintings, and famous quotes.

11. SWEET GROUPS

During holiday periods, there is usually a large supply of candies available that are wrapped in different colored foils. These provide excellent vehicles for forming random groups. In a box, put equal amounts of each color of wrapped candy to correspond to the number of students you want in each group. (For example, if you want five groups of four students each, put four candies with red wrappers, four with gold, four with green, four with silver, and four striped.) Mix the candies and have each student select one from the box without looking. Have the students form groups in which all the candies are wrapped in the same colored wrapper. Tell them they may eat the candy as soon as they are in their groups and ready to begin.

12. STUDENT CHOICE

Ask the students to form groups of the size you desire and let them choose with whom they will group. This is an excellent approach at the beginning of a school year or class. It provides a safe way to let the students know they will be working in groups and gets them used to it before the tasks become more difficult. We would recommend groups of no more than three in the beginning.

13. TRIVIAL PURSUIT

Prepare two sets of 3x5 cards – one set with questions and the other set with the answers to these questions. The lower the level of the question, the easier this grouping task will be, but the less challenging also. Give each student a card, making sure that the question and answer pairs have been distributed. Direct the students who have the questions to find their answer partners. Duplicate copies of particular questions or answers can be used to address the possible problem of having an odd number of students.

5.14   NON-VERBAL COMMUNICATION

PURPOSE

To increase awareness of non-verbal communication through mirroring non-verbal behaviors.

DESCRIPTION

Much of communication is non-verbal. Many students are not aware of the non-verbal messages they're sending, and others are not aware of how they're picking up some messages. This is a fun and active way of heightening students' awareness of non-verbal communication.

USES

Group Effectiveness

PROCEDURE

1. Have the students choose partners. For this activity, do not force unwanted partnerships, and protect all students from embarrassment.

2. Ask each partnership to decide who will be the leader and who will be the follower for the first round of the activity. (Some people refer to the follower as the "mirror.") Tell the students their roles will reverse later for a second round.

3. Advise the partnerships that each round will last three minutes. (As the activity progresses, monitor the partnerships carefully. Shorten the time if need be to protect any pair from undue embarrassment).

4. Tell the students that when you say go, the leaders are to make deliberate movements that the followers are to mimic as closely as they can. Advise the leaders to start with movements that are slow enough that the follower can mimic them. Also direct the students to keep their movements to those that are acceptable for the classroom.

5. After the allotted time, ask them to quickly switch roles.

6. Facilitate a debriefing. Encourage the students to be free in discussing their feelings.

Grade Level: Elementary, Middle, High School

Time: 10 minutes

Motivational Standards: Involving, Enabling

Pluses: Block Schedules, Group Processing, Multiple Intelligences

5.15   READY CARDS FOR GROUP WORK

Make it easier to manage group timing with ready cards. Have each group fold a 5 x 7 card in half to make a tent. Have them write READY in large letters on one side of the tent, and WORKING on the other. When using group activities, have the groups use their ready cards to indicate when they're ready for the next step.

QUICK TIP

5.16   WRAP-UPS

PURPOSE

To provide for group reflection, self-assessment, and growth.

DESCRIPTION

After any group activity, it is important to deliberately plan for reflection. Here are two ways this can be done.

USES

Group Effectiveness

GROUP WRAP UPS:

One of the simplest is to ask the groups to develop a group response to questions such as . . .

  • Three things we did really well are . . .   We know each of these because . . .

- One way we could have worked even better together . . . To do this next time, each of us will . . .

- What was most interesting about what we did was . . . We think so because . . .

- Ways we can use what we're learning are . . .

- What each of us did best was . . .

- A commitment each of us has made is . . .

INDIVIDUAL WRAP-UPS

This is similar to the strategy *Door Passes* in Chapter four. Have each student complete an individual wrap-up by responding to a given prompt on a sheet of paper. Allow the students to respond by any of the following methods:

- draw a picture,

- write a poem or limerick,

- list thoughts,

- write a paragraph, or

- any effective means.

Possible prompts . . .

- What I liked best was . . .

- What I did best was . . .

- What I learned was . . .

- A way I will work better in the group next time is . . .

- What my group did best was . . .

- The way I feel about what we accomplished is . . .

Grade Level: Elementary, Middle, High School

Time: 5-10 minutes

Motivational Standards: Involving

Pluses: Block Schedules, Group Processing

CHAPTER 6

SELF-REFLECTION AND

ASSESSMENT PROMPTS

QUESTIONS AND PROMPTS TO ENCOURAGE AND FACILITATE
ASSESSMENT OF BEHAVIORS, THOUGHT PROCESSES, AND
IMPROVEMENT EFFORTS

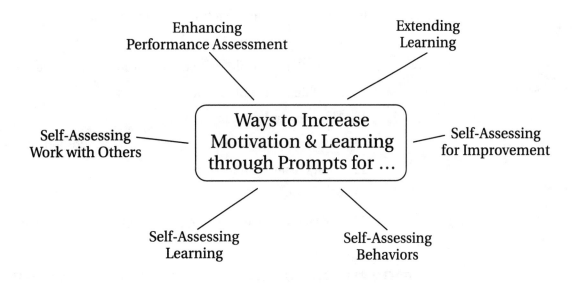

ASSESSMENT PROMPTS

Reprinted with permission from *The High Performance Toolbox*
(© 1997-1998, Peak Learning Systems, Inc.)

Use these prompts before, during, or after important learning and assessment situations to foster reflection, self-assessment and improvement.

PROMPTS FOR SELF-EXTENDING LEARNING

1. How might I apply this learning, connection, or application to a new context?

2. How might I use what I have learned in the future?

3. I can use what I have learned to do when I …

4. I used to think … but now I know …

5. I was on the right track with my idea about … but what I didn't know was …

6. What will be the benefits of continuing to use what I have learned?

7. What might happen if …?

8. A question I am curious about and want to find the answer to is …

9. One thing I am not sure of …

10. Three things I wonder about …

11. What am I curious about and/or what am I confused about?

12. What I really want to learn is …

13. What have I learned that I can continue to use?

14. The new questions that arose during today's lesson or activities are …

PROMPTS FOR ENHANCING PERFORMANCE ASSESSMENTS

(Several of the prompts in this section were contributed by John Booth of the Glendale Union High School District in Glendale, Arizona.)

1. Explain why you used the procedures you did.

2. Describe the process you used.

3. Explain how you ...

4. Explain why you ...

5. Support your decision/conclusion/recommendation.

6. What conclusions can be drawn from your work? Justify your conclusions.

7. What predictions can be made based on your work/findings? Justify your findings.

8. What recommendations can be made based on your findings? Support your recommendations with a convincing argument.

9. Explain why your findings are what they are.

10. How can what you've done in this situation be used in ____ (another similar situation)? Explain how and why.

11. What might happen differently if ... ?

12. How can you conclude that ... ?

13. Explain how _____ (situation) is similar to _____ (a similar situation).

14. Propose an alternative, but rational, procedure for solving a given problem. Which procedure is best and why?

15. Present another problem that could be solved by the process you used. Explain how you would use it and why it is appropriate.

16. How would/might it have turned out differently if ...? Support your conclusion.

17. How do you know that ... ? (... is the best? ... is the worst? ...is the most likely? ... is a sound conclusion? ... is reasonable? ... is true?)

PROMPTS FOR SELF-ASSESSING WHAT'S BEEN LEARNED

1. How accurate is the information I have found?

2. I use what I've learned to do to ...

3. What more information do I need in order to ...?

4. What did I learn to do this week?

5. What did I learn well enough to teach a friend?

6. The skills I need to refine are ...

7. I refine my _____ skills by ...

8. One thing I learned today was ...

9. What did I learn to do from what I did?

10. What did I learn to do that I did not know before?

11. What is the most important learning, connection, or application I gained during this lesson or unit?

12. Today my thinking is like the animal … because both …

13. Today my thinking is like the color … because both …

14. How can what I learned benefit me now?

PROMPTS FOR SELF-ASSESSING LEARNING BEHAVIORS

1. What skills do I need in order to …?

2. What were the effects of what I did?

3. What were the effects of what I did best?

4. How did I approach this new learning situation in order to maximize my learning?

5. How did I do it?

6. How well did I do … and how can I do even better?

7. It was hard for me to learn …

8. When I get stuck _____ (reading, writing, adding, spelling, etc.), I …

9. The most important thing I have learned about learning this week is …

10. What caused me to achieve this learning, connection, or application?

11. What caused or aided my learning?

12. What do I do when I think about my thinking?

13. What helped me to learn _____ was …

14. I adjusted for how I learn best by …

PROMPTS FOR SELF-ASSESSING WORK WITH OTHERS

1. What did I do to be a good listener?

2. What did I do when I worked with others to better the group effort?

3. What can I do to work better with others?

4. When I worked with others, what I did best was … I know this because …

PROMPTS FOR SELF- ASSESSMENT AND IMPROVEMENT

1. How have I modeled the characteristics of a self-directed learner?

2. How will I show that I have kept my promise to do even better next time?

3. What can I celebrate?

4. What caused my success?

5. What will I promise to myself to help me do even better in the future?

6. The ways I have improved are …

7. How close did I come to reaching my goal?

8. What have I done to try and improve in my goal area?

9. Is it necessary to make adjustments in my goals? Why or why not?

10. My greatest strength in the area of _____ is … (support with specific examples)

11. My greatest weakness in the area of _____ is … (support with specific examples)

12. This is an explanation of how I did my work …

13. I planned what I did by …

14. I used the feedback I received throughout the process by …

15. I did my best work today when I …

16. I know my work was done well because …

17. The best part of my work is … The evidence I have to support this is …

18. I am most proud of _____ because …

19. How effective was it when …?

20. How efficient was it when …?

21. I know _____ is excellent because …

22. What more needs to be done?

23. I can make my work even better by …

24. If I were going to do this again, the changes I would make are … because …

25. My _____ would be more logical if I …

26. My _____ would be more convincing if …

27. In order to be more persuasive, I could …

28. In order for my _____ to be more complete and thorough, I need to …

29. If I could revise _____, I would …

30. How can I _____ more effectively next time?

31. How can I _____ more efficiently next time?

32. In order to be more effective, it is necessary to …

33. In order to be more efficient, it is necessary to …

34. In order to be more solution oriented, I could …

35. In order to get better results next time, I will …

CHAPTER 7

PROJECTS, PRODUCTS, AND PERFORMANCE IDEAS

HUNDREDS OF IDEAS FOR IMPROVING THE RICHNESS,
RELEVANCE, MEANINGFUL OPTIONS, AND INTEREST WITH STUDENTS

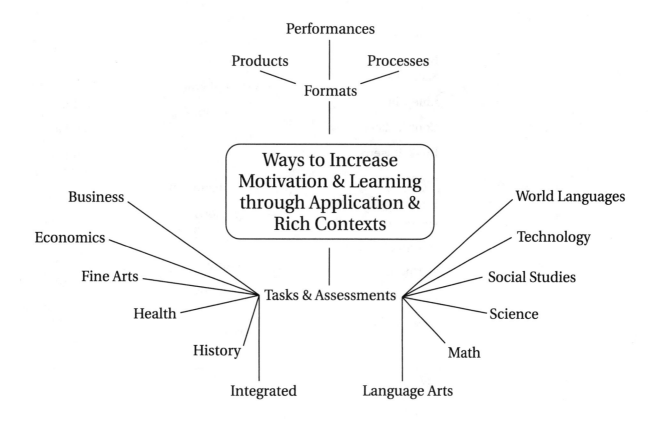

PRODUCT AND PERFORMANCE IDEAS

Reprinted with permission from *The High Performance Toolbox* (© 1997, Peak Learning Systems, Inc.)

Advertisements

Analogies

Anecdotes and Stories

Art Exhibits

Art Fairs

Articles (Journals, Magazine, Newspaper, etc.)

Audio Tapes

Autobiographies

Ballads

Banners

Biographical Sketches

Blueprints

Book Jackets

Book Reviews

Brochures

Bulletin Board Displays

Bumper Stickers

Cartoons

Cartoon Strips

Case Studies

Charts

Children's Books

Classified Ads

Clothes Design

Coat of Arms

Collages

Comic Books

Commentaries

Commercials (Radio & TV)

Computer Discs (CD's)

Computer Programs

Concept Maps

Conventions

Dances

Debates

Demonstrations

Depictions

Diaries

Dioramas

Documentaries

Dramatic Presentations

Dramatic Readings

Editorials

Essays

Ethnic Dishes or Meals

Exhibitions

Fact Sheets

Fairy Tales

Family Trees

Fishbone Charts

Flags

Flow Charts

Folk Tales

Games

Globes

Graphs

Graphic Organizers

Graffiti Wall

Guess Who or What Descriptions

Hieroglyphics

Historical "You Are There" Scenes

Home Pages

Hyperlearning Stack

Icons

Illustrations

Instructions and Advice

Interviews

Journals

Lab Reports

Last Will and Testaments

Lectures

Letters (Personal & Professional)

Limericks

Logos

Logs

Magazines

Maps (Geographic, Weather, & Treasure)

Matrices

Memos

Metaphors

Models

Mobiles

Mock Trials

Monologues

Montages

Mottoes and Slogans

Movies

Murals

Museum Displays

Music Videos

Musical Composition

Newsletters

Newspapers

Notes

Nursery Rhymes

Obituaries

Oral Presentations

Outlines

Paintings

Pamphlets

Panel Discussions

Pantomimes

Parodies

Patterns

-Descriptive

-Cause/Effect

-Generalization

-Sequence

-Solution

Photo Displays

Photo Journals with Captions

Pictographs

Pictorials

Plans

Plays

Poems

Political Rallies

"Pop Up" Books

Portfolios

Poster Displays

Presentations (Formal & Informal)

Proposals

Puppet Show

Puzzles

Quizzes

Radio Broadcasts

Recipes

Recitals

Reenactments of Historical Events

Reports

Research Papers

Resumes and Cover Letters

Reviews (TV, Movie, etc.)

Role Plays

Schedules

Science Fiction

Science Demonstrations

Science Projects

Scrapbooks

Scripts

Scrolls

Sculptures

"Show and Tell"

Short Stories

Set Designs (TV & Theater)

Simulations

Sketches

Skits

Slide Shows

Soap Operas

Software with Documentation

Songs

Sonnets

Speech (Formal & Extemporaneous)

Spread Sheets

Story Boxes

Story Maps

Story Problems

Summaries

Surveys

Talk Shows (TV & Radio)

Teaching Lessons

Technical Reports

Telegrams

"Thumbnail" Sketches

Time Capsules

Timelines

Trade Shows

Travel Guides

Tribute or Eulogy

T-shirts

TV Programs

Venn Diagrams

Videos

Voter's Guides

Wall Hangings

Webs

Web Pages

Web Sites

Work Samples

Word Searches

PERFORMANCE IDEAS

Reprinted with permission from *The High Performance Toolbox* (© 1997-1998, Peak Learning Systems, Inc.)

1. PERFORMANCE IDEAS FOR ALL AREAS & GRADE LEVELS

1. Design, construct, and use a teaching museum.

2. Develop "How to ....." manuals and handbooks.

3. Write a note to a friend explaining or describing a concept or skill.

4. Develop a supported projection as response to, "What would happen if ...?"

5. Explain or describe something through a metaphor. Defend your metaphor based on similarities of multiple characteristics and functions.

6. Create and use an educational game to teach significant information.

7. Create simulations showing real-life applications of a concept or competence.

8. Create and defend concept maps and/or other organized charts and patterns.

9. Explain/describe a complex concept - checking and adjusting to be certain the audience understands.

10. Determine or choose ill-defined problems - determine best possible solutions.

11. Analyze attributes of famous people in your discipline - then create and role play a great person showing how he/she has/can benefit others.

12. Find, portray, and explain applications of concepts, procedures, or processes in your community.

13. Build and use a diorama to teach a meaningful concept.

14. Create and use depictions of complex concepts, issues, connections.

15. Create questions, tasks, and rubrics that will prove someone can do or understand something. Use them for self and/or peer assessment.

16. Design role plays and simulations for a purpose relevant to others.

17. Design and build models for a purpose relevant to others.

18. Create and lead self-assessment conferences (student-led conferences) based on portfolios showing evidence of status and growth with specific outcomes.

19. Design, do, and defend quizzes, tests, assessments, and performances.

20. Explain/describe the process for something.

21. Create and present a personal poster showing who you are, what you're proud of, and what your goals are.

22. Design and do a research project for a relevant purpose.

23. Write songs that convey significant messages.

24. Maintain portfolios showing evidence of self-assessment, best work, and/or growth.

25. As a class, develop quality standards for work and behavior based on a careful study of exemplary models.

26. Analyze for commonalties and differences - draw conclusions based on findings.

27. Find and disprove misperceptions.

28. Regularly summarize into sentences "most significant or usable learnings."

29. Create and explain a flow chart for important procedures or processes.

30. Develop, defend, and respond appropriately to questions that are appropriate differentiators for Advanced Placement Exams or other standardized exams.

31. Design and display a mural/billboard to ...   Explain and justify your work.

32. Teach significant concepts to others (e.g., parents, younger students, peers, etc.).

33. Identify community and/or environmental problems - then research or design experiments to determine and justify best possible solutions.

34. Design, create, and publish a study guide.

35. Develop and use consensus building skills in authentic situations.

36. Determine how subject matter is used by local professionals and present to younger students.

37. Find and present applications of what is being taught in the physical world.

38. Document the improvement in your _____ efforts in a portfolio that includes specific evidence of your performance levels over the last eight weeks. In a letter to your portfolio reader, identify the specific evidence in your portfolio that shows the improvements you have achieved.

39. Based on at least three sources, develop and share a report on a given topic for the purpose of informing others.

40. Create and publish a newsletter with reflections and predictions.

41. Create an advertising campaign.

42. Work through a given problem or procedure, being careful to show each step. Write a description of each step and explain why you did it. Justify the reasonableness of your answer.

43. Discern patterns, explain or describe them, and explain how they can be used.

44. Using a current issue, research the quality of information available on the Internet. Make justified recommendations to a curriculum committee.

45. Create an interactive Worldwide Web Site to provide reliable, usable, and significant information on a specific topic.

46. Investigate causes of accidents on the playground. Propose solutions to reduce these accidents.

2. MAJOR INTERDISCIPLINARY PERFORMANCES

1. Collect news reports from overseas and, in groups, work to produce an international newspaper that reflects the perspectives represented by different countries. When possible, compare and contrast the perspectives in foreign countries with those in the United States.

2. Produce a well supported recommendation to consumers based on a study of "truth in advertising."

3. Write and share or perform stories/plays around real-world problems and solutions.

4. Based on a survey of at least 20 students and 10 parents of children between the ages of 5 and 10, determine the predominant position in your sample toward regulating violence in cartoons on Saturday mornings. Develop and present a position paper to be presented to your local television station that represents this predominant position and supports it using the constitution and recent court rulings.

5. Create and operate a micro-society.

3. LANGUAGE ARTS

1. Produce an orientation video for new students.

2. Use writing, speech, music, and photos to present family folklore.

3. Develop and share children's stories that convey a relevant message.

4. In writing or speech, summarize a piece of significant non-fiction writing in order to convey the essential points to a specific audience.

5. Select a particular topic and find examples of presentations in different media concerning that topic. Identify the media that you feel best serves the topic and justify your selection.

6. Develop and explain a visual which compares/contrasts characters in literature with people you actually know.

7. Research children's literature in order to identify the salient characteristics. Interview young children to identify what they like about professionally produced children's books. Then, create an original children's story that adheres to the findings of your research. Share your story with young readers and if possible have them either illustrate your story or at least help you with the illustrations.

8. Develop and present a visual biographical timeline.

9. Create an audio tape of the most important sounds in your life. Write a narrative describing the sounds and exploring their importance to you.

10. Write a descriptive essay about a family heirloom or tradition of special significance. Include your selection in the class book entitled *What It Means To Be A Family*.

4. SOCIAL STUDIES

1. Publish and distribute a voter's guide.

2. Create simulations of historical/cultural interactions, problems, and solutions. Share supported conclusions that are still relevant today.

3. Create and perform a "You Are There" program conveying supported recommendations based on past and present connections.

4. Prepare for and conduct a trial regarding a current issue.

5. Identify the information about the city in which you live that would be most important or of great interest to someone considering moving into your area. Create a pamphlet that highlights your information, and share it with members of city government in hopes that they might officially distribute it through their office.

6. Develop and display an historical depiction of your town using letters, interviews, photographs, researched text, and other documents.

7. Research and present how a conflict (such as in the Middle East) is affected by culture, ethnicity, economics, and geography.

8. Select a state and create a public service presentation. The purpose of this project is to encourage people to come to your state to vacation or to do business. Your presentation should highlight information about the state that you deem important and should be supported with appropriate visuals.

9. Research a topic related to immigration and present a display representing your findings to an appropriate audience.

10. Describe how to locate a place on a map/globe when given longitude and latitude.

5. INCORPORATING LANGUAGE ARTS AND SOCIAL STUDIES

1. Put a famous person in history on trial in light of what is known today (e.g., Harry Truman).

2. Develop a position and support it with music, art, an historical event, and poetry.

3. Take famous quotes and explain why they are still important.

4. Identify and research a famous historical personality in order to role-play that person. Write a biographical entry and present yourself to your classmates/parents. Clearly portray your historical contributions. Identify what have been significant effects of your life's contributions on today's society – explain and justify your thoughts.

5. Write a modern day myth that incorporates what we have learned in our study of mythology. Then explain what your myth reveals about mankind and society today.

6. Research a current topic, write an article that accurately reflects your findings, write an editorial, and draw an editorial cartoon.

7. Using published cartoons as a central vehicle, present a position and support for it.

8. Use at least five persuasion techniques in either writing or speaking to endorse a position; assess the effectiveness of your efforts and explain why you used the techniques the way you did based on the conditions inherent in the task.

9. In writing or speech, express a conclusion regarding an issue based on the results of comparing, contrasting, and evaluating the points of view of two authors or speakers.

10. Recreate an historical period. (Identify and explain connections - then make predictions based on patterns).

11. Compare a literary representation of an historical period to actual documented information (e.g., *The Grapes of Wrath* - The Great Depression). Present your supported opinions as to why there is or is not a discrepancy concerning …

12. "Create an original drama showcasing the dominant philosophies, artistic works, occupations, and social class distinctions of an historical period" (From the State of Minnesota).

13. Compare/Contrast information about an event in the news with information about the same topic from a different medium such as magazine, documentary film, or Internet (an attack by the United States on Iraq). Support your conclusions regarding similarities and differences.

14. Studying a period in history through the eyes of a child can present a very interesting and sometimes very surprising point of view. Become a child during WWII and write a diary in which you record how and why the events of the war affected your life. A few perspectives that might prove interesting are children in the Resistance, children of Oriental heritage living in California, children living in Pearl Harbor, Hiroshima, or London during the bombings.

15. Assume the role of a newspaper reporter in 1862. You have been given the assignment of interviewing one of the women or men who have journeyed westward and settled in the new territories. The newspaper wants you to submit a "human interest" article by describing what life was like for these people and by sharing your conclusions about gender roles during westward expansion.

6. INCORPORATING LANGUAGE ARTS, SOCIAL STUDIES, AND MATH

1. Publish a newsletter portraying inaccurate perceptions being created currently through misuses of statistical procedures.

2. Study a wide range of magazines, newspapers, televised commentaries, and the like. Identify several issues of interest, watch and read widely about these issues, chart the various viewpoints on each issue, and discuss the information supporting each. Prepare a media guide for one of the issues.

7. TECHNOLOGY

1. Develop, draw, and model ideas for the use of space in a mode of living that is out of the ordinary - a tree house, a space station, an underwater dwelling, etcetera.

2. Research and evaluate ideas for "adaptive devices" that can make life easier for persons with disabilities. Based on your findings, make recommendations for improvements to the device or ways to extend its usefulness.

3. Provide evidence showing a specific technological innovation has impacted the environment.

4. Construct a model of a technological device or system and describe how it has contributed to or hindered human progress.

5. Develop applications for available software and/or other technologies.

6. Use the documentation for a software package to learn how to use a procedure. Provide evidence that you learned the procedure and how to apply it. The procedure needs to be one NOT taught in class or previously known.

7. Develop and implement a plan to reduce water and energy consumption in your classroom or home.

8. Research your city plat documents, select a specific, available site, and design a house that meets all applicable codes and that aesthetically complements the landscape.

8. INCORPORATING TECHNOLOGY AND SOCIAL STUDIES

1. Create and produce a segment for a TV commentary that compares information about a specific time period in a social studies textbook with information contained in diaries from the same period (e.g., Civil War, WW II, Depression, etc.).

2. Select several specific places in the world and research how architecture reflects the geographic locations. Present your findings with appropriate visuals.

3. Research your city's past urban design and create a model that accurately depicts your findings. Gather information about your city's present urban plan and compare this with your model. Based on the results of your comparison, write an article for the local paper that predicts what the city's urban design will look like in 75 to 100 years. Support your predictions using trends in your area and elsewhere.

9. INCORPORATING TECHNOLOGY AND SCIENCE

1. "Compile a case study of a technological development that has had a significant impact on the environment and report the findings to an appropriate audience" (From the New York State Department of Education).

2. "Choose materials based upon their acoustic properties to make a set of wind chimes" (From the New York State Department of Education). Explain your design and material selection.

3. Build a model to test an hypothesis.

10. INCORPORATING TECHNOLOGY, SCIENCE, AND LANGUAGE ARTS

1. "Describe, through example, how familiar technologies can have positive and negative impacts on the environment and on the way people live and work" (From the New York State Department of Education). Make recommendations based on the findings.

11. SCIENCE

1. "Relate physical characteristics of organisms to habitat characteristics (e.g., long hair and fur color change for mammals living in cold climates)" (From the New York State Department of Education).

2. Identify and describe applications of physics principles in everyday life.

3. Build "models" in the community that teach difficult to perceive subject matter to the public. For example, build a scale representation that shows distances within the solar system. Develop and present supporting information that explains and justifies what has been built.

4. Design, execute, document, and report on an experiment.

5. Teach middle school students about chemical reactions using information and examples that are relevant to early teens.

6. Develop a landscape plan for a member of the community. The plan must be based on the expressed tastes, needs, and resources of the person and on the environmental needs and conditions of the region.

7. Design an experiment to show at what angle a three foot ramp should be placed to cause a marble that rolls down it to then roll the greatest distance across the floor. Describe, conduct, and report on your efforts.

8. Create a life form (simulated) for a given environment. Justify your conclusion.

9. Acting in the role of a particular species (e.g., grizzly bear), publish a newsletter that reports regularly on different regions and the advantages and disadvantages to you of living in or visiting these places.

12. INCORPORATING SCIENCE AND LANGUAGE ARTS

1. Develop, through research, a proposal to test a hypothesis of a given concept. Submit the proposal to an appropriate panel of judges who will rate the proposal on clarity, appropriateness, and feasibility.

2. Research a planet and create an imaginary life form that could exist in that environment. Interview the "creature" about life on the planet and write an article for the human interest section of the Sunday paper.

13. INCORPORATING SCIENCE, LANGUAGE ARTS, AND SOCIAL STUDIES

1. Adopt an endangered species and develop and share an analysis of the advantages and disadvantages of protecting or not protecting it.

2. "Investigate the effects of alterations on cultural and/or physical landscapes (e.g., construction of a mall, changes in local traffic patterns, rezoning from residential to commercial, etc.) in order to develop recommendations for how to maximize benefits and minimize disadvantages" (From the State of Minnesota).

14. MATH

1. Design a cardboard package that is most economical for given dimensions and weights of the intended contents. Justify your design.

2. Determine with justification whether contestants on "Let's Make a Deal" should stick with their first choice or switch to a new door after they are shown what's behind one of the doors.

3. Examine and analyze tabularly presented data in order to create representative graphs - then make and defend predictions based on the trends in the data.

4. The school is interested in knowing exactly how much tile it will take when the floor is retiled. Determine the square footage necessary, and the number of nine inch square tiles that will be needed if

there is about a two percent waste factor. Use written text and diagrams to describe your procedures.

5. Postal rates have been figured by the ounce since July 1, 1885. Here are the rates for the past 62 years: . . . Based on the postal rates since 1932, predict the cost of mailing a one ounce first class letter in 2001. When, if ever, do you think the cost will be $1.00? Explain your reasoning.

6. Assuming the earth's population will continue to increase at the same rate it is today, how long will it be until the earth will probably not be able to produce enough food for everyone? Present your findings in the form of a school science advisory.

7. Use a motion detector and a TI 82 calculator to develop graphical representations showing the relationships between distance, rate, and time.

8. Estimate the number of blades of grass in your lawn using appropriate statistical procedures.

9. Design and produce a quilt pattern and describe its symmetry. Put all of the class patterns together and display your quilt in an appropriate area.

10. Determine how many people are in attendance at a major event by sampling areas within a photograph.

15. INCORPORATING MATH AND SCIENCE

1. Many people believe J.F. Kennedy was shot by someone on the grassy knoll. Prove or disprove the shot from the *grassy knoll theory* using physics, mathematics, and publicly available archives.

2. Make a record of reported earthquakes and volcanoes during the past 20 years. Identify and interpret the pattern formed worldwide. Report your findings and interpretations through the use of appropriate graphics. Make predictions based on observed trends.

16. INCORPORATING MATH AND LANGUAGE ARTS

1. Given data on graphs, write a story that represents the data or graph.

2. Given headlines or claims with background data, explain whether or not the claims are reasonable.

17. INCORPORATING MATH AND TECHNOLOGY

1. "Build a city skyline to demonstrate skill in linear measurements, scale drawing, ratio, fractions, angles, and geometric shapes." (New York State Department of Education).

2. For actual maintenance projects being planned at your school, research the projects in order to determine the specific amount of materials and resources necessary to complete the projects.

3. Plan a city, including efficient road networks, garbage collection and mail routings, plans for voting processes and equitable precincts. Develop and present a paper that explains the mathematics and design decisions. The paper is also to provide rationale to support the selection of your plans by a company wishing to construct a planned community.

18. INCORPORATING MATH, SCIENCE, AND TECHNOLOGY

1. Find places in our community where the concepts we have been studying are being used or exist. Determine why each of the concepts was used the way it was or why each is an example of the concept. Put together a picture/drawing album showing the application and the reason why it is an application. Use your album to teach younger students the reasons why what we're learning is important.

2. Given trends or sample data, make and justify predictions.

19. INCORPORATING MATH, SCIENCE, TECHNOLOGY, AND SOCIAL STUDIES

1. Given multiple or competing interpretations of certain data, justify each interpretation.

2. Make predictions based on the identification and analysis of trends.

20. INCORPORATING MATH AND SOCIAL STUDIES

1. Refer to the attached charts and graphs distributed by various political candidates. Determine how the charts actually misrepresent the data. In writing, explain how the misrepresentations are created. Also, describe how the charts should be done to accurately reflect the data. Explain the potential disadvantage to the voters in inaccurately interpreting the data.

21. INCORPORATING MATH, SOCIAL STUDIES, AND SCIENCE

1. Use sampling to determine, track, and predict the population of a targeted entity within an environment.

22. INCORPORATING BUSINESS AND TECHNOLOGY

1. Create, produce, and market a product.

2. Interview people in the community about job possibilities and responsibilities. Create a database of careers in your community and present to an appropriate audience.

23. INCORPORATING BUSINESS AND ECONOMICS

1. Analyze, interpret, and evaluate family financial structures and procedures in order to create and defend a family financial structure and the procedures by which it will function.

2. "Compare several retirement investment strategies and propose with justification the one you think is most appropriate for an adult you know." (From the State of Minnesota).

3. Compare and contrast marketing in a traditional store with a discount store. Present your findings to a board of local business people.

24. WORLD LANGUAGES

1. Use your knowledge of one language to interpret common written communication in another, unknown language.

25. INCORPORATING WORLD LANGUAGES AND SOCIAL STUDIES

1. Create travel brochures, including recommendations for inter-cultural interactions.

2. Portray conditions, issues, or recommendations in a target language.

3. Select a country and do research on the customs and beliefs of that country. Examine official tourist brochures and articles containing interviews with different classes of residents. Then produce a report that compares and contrasts the different views.

4. Simulate functioning effectively under contextual conditions within a single culture or between multiple cultures.

5. Your family has been selected to serve as a host family for a student from ___. Research the country and the specific area where your exchange student lives. Also, identify and study specific cultural items you think you and your family need to know before your new "family member" arrives. Put your findings, along with supported recommendations, into a written report for your family.

26. INCORPORATING HEALTH AND PHYSICAL EDUCATION

1. Develop a diet that utilizes best available information for a particular person.

2. Design and implement a personal wellness program.

3. Design a research supported wellness program that is custom tailored for a relative. In your plan, address fitness, exercise, nutrition, and motivation.

4. Create a presentation about the correlation between employee fitness to job performance, absenteeism, and emotional stability. Present your findings to the appropriate audience, being sure to include viable recommendations and plans for a healthier work environment.

5. Create a public service video that promotes positive behavioral choices concerning drugs, alcohol, and/or tobacco.

6. Investigate an important health issue and evaluate its impact on members of your community (e.g., contamination of the city water supply).

27. FINE ARTS

1. Use the fine arts to raise local awareness of current issues.

2. Use the fine arts to convey or persuade.

3. Tell a story through an original dance sequence.

4. Research logo and flag design. Develop a logo and flag for your cooperative team. Present your designs to the class and justify your design rationale.

5. Investigate an art object or a piece of architecture and explain how the artist/architect used design elements or principles to express an idea or feeling.

6. Design a statue, monument, or piece of art for a specific public space and a specific purpose. Explain your choice of media, imagery, purpose, and location.

7. Create a mural that shows ways people demonstrate friendship. Write a narrative that describes what has been depicted in the mural.

ADDITIONAL RESOURCES

Armstrong, Thomas. *Multiple Intelligences in the Classroom.* ASCD, 1994.

Armstrong, Thomas. *7 Kinds of Smart: Identifying and Developing Your Many Intelligences.* Plume, 1993.

Belasco, James A. and Ralph C. Stayer. *Flight Of The Buffalo.* Warner Books, 1993.

Berliner, David C. and Bruce J. Biddle. *The Manufactured Crises.* Addison Wesley, 1995.

Block, James H., Helen E. Efthim, and Robert B. Burns. *Building Effective Mastery Learning Schools.* Longman, Inc., 1989.

Buzan, Tony. *Use Both Sides of Your Brain.* 3rd edition. Plume, 1991.

Canady, Robert Lynn and Michael D. Rettig. *Block Scheduling: A Catalyst for Change in High Schools.* Eye On Education, 1995.

Csikszentmihalyi, Mihaly. *Flow – The Psychology of Optimal Experience.* Harper Perennial, 1990.

Covey, Stephen R. *Principle Centered Leadership.* Summit Books, 1990, 1991.

Covey, Stephen R. *The 7 Seven Habits of Highly Effective People.* Simon and Schuster, 1989.

Creative Training Techniques Newsletter. Lakewood Publications, (800) 707-7749.

DePorter, Bobbi with Mike Hernacki. *Quantum Learning: Unleashing the Genius in You.* Dell Publishing, 1992.

Gardner, Howard. *Frames of Mind.* Basic Books, 1983.

Gardner, Howard. *Multiple Intelligences.* Basic Books, 1993.

Garmston, Robert J. and Bruce M. Wellman. *How to Make Presentations that Teach and Transform.* ASCD, 1992.

Glasser, William. *Control Theory in the Classroom.* Harper and Rowe, 1986.

Glasser, William. *The Quality School: Managing Students Without Coercion.* Harper & Row, 1990.

Goleman, Daniel. *Emotional Intelligence.* Bantam, 1995.

Gusky, Thomas R. *Implementing Mastery Learning.* Wadsworth, Inc., 1985.

Harmin, Merrill. *Inspiring Active Learning: A Handbook for Teachers.* ASCD, 1994.

Harrison, Ann Salisbury and Francis Burton Spuler. *Hot Tips for Teachers.* Fearon Teacher Aids, Simon & Schuster Supplementary Education Group, 1983.

Hendricks, William ... [et. al.] *Secrets of Power Presentations.* Career Press, 1996.

Hyerle, David. *Visual Tools for Constructing Knowledge.* ASCD, 1996.

Jensen, Eric. *Brain-Based Learning.* Turning Point Publishing, 1996.

Jensen, Eric. *Super Teaching.* Turning Point Publishing, 1995.

Jensen, Eric. *The Learning Brain.* Turning Point Publishing, 1995.

Kagan, Spencer. *Cooperative Learning.* Kagan Cooperative Learning, 1992, 1994.

Kohn, Alfie. *Beyond Discipline: From Compliance to Community.* ASCD, 1996.

Mamchur, Carolyn. *A Teacher's Guide to Cognitive Type Theory & Learning Style.* ASCD, 1996.

Margulies, Nancy. *Mapping Inner Space.* Zephyr Press, 1991.

Marzano, Robert J. *A Different Kind of Classroom: Teaching with Dimensions of Learning.* ASCD, 1992.

Marzano, Robert J., Pickering, Debra J. ... [et. al.] *Dimensions of Learning.* ASCD, 1992.

Marzano, Robert J., Pickering, Debra J. ... [et. al.] *Implementing Dimensions of Learning.* ASCD, 1992.

McCombs, Barbara L. and James E. Pope. *Motivating Hard to Reach Students.* American Psychological Association, 1994.

McPhee, Doug. *Limitless Learning: Making Powerful Learning an Everday Event.* Zephyr Press, 1996.

Newstom, John W. and Edward E. Scannell. *Games Trainers Play.* McGraw Hill, 1980.

Nilson, Carolyn. *Team Games for Trainers.* McGraw Hill, 1993.

Oakley, Ed and Doug Krug. *Enlightened Leadership.* Simon & Schuster, 1991.

Raffini, James P. *150 Ways to Increase Intrinsic Motivation in the Classroom,* Allyn & Bacon, 1996.

Richards, Regina G. *Learn: Playful Techniques to Accelerate Learning.* Zephyr Press, 1993.

Ridley, Dale Scott and Bill Walther. *Creating Responsible Learners.* American Psychological Association, 1995.

Rogers, Spence and Shari Graham. *The High Performance Toolbox: Succeeding with Performance Tasks, Projects, and Assessments.* Peak Learning Systems, 1997.

Rose, Colin. *Accelerated Learning.* Accelerated Learning Systems, Ltd., 1985.

Scannell, Edward E. and John W. Newstom. *More Games Trainers Play.* McGraw Hill, 1983.

Scannell, Edward E. and John W. Newstom. *Still More Games Trainers Play.* McGraw Hill, 1991.

Seligman, Martin E.P. *Learned Optimism.* Pocket Books, 1992.

Senge, Peter M. *The Fifth Discipline.* Doubleday - Currency, 1990.

Sternberg, Robert J. and Williams, Wendy M. *How to Develop Student Creativity.* ASCD, 1996.

Stiggins, Richard J. *Student-Centered Classroom Assessment.* Merrill, 1994.

Sylwester, Robert. *A Celebration of Neurons: An Educator's Guide to the Human Brain.* ASCD, 1995.

Wheatley, Margaret J. *Leadership and the New Science.* Berrett-Koehler, 1992,1994.

Wiggins, Grant P. *Assessing Student Performance.* Jossey-Bass, 1993.

Wlodkowski, Raymond J. *Enhancing Adult Motivation to Learn.* Jossey-Bass, 1985.

Wlodkowski, Raymond J. and Margery B. Ginsberg. *Diversity and Motivation.* Jossey-Bass, 1995.

INDEX

H, I

S

T, U, V, W, X, Y, Z

ORDERING INFORMATION

RESOURCES FROM PEAK LEARNING SYSTEMS

The High Performance Toolbox: Succeeding with Performance Tasks, Projects, and Assessments by Spence Rogers and Shari Graham

Practical, teacher-tested guidelines, templates, strategies, tips and supporting examples for successfully using performance tasks and assessments as a part of a comprehensive approach to student learning and achievement.

Motivation & Learning: A Teacher's Guide to Building Excitement for Learning and Igniting the Drive for Quality by Spence Rogers, Jim Ludington, and Shari Graham

Over 600 immediately usable ideas, strategies and tips with a supporting theoretical foundation to improve the quality of motivation, achievement, and student work.

High Performance Toolbox Duplication Masters

Over 50, ready-to-use duplication masters of critical templates to support individual users of *The High Performance Toolbox* book. Site licenses are available for considerable savings.

Motivation & Learning Duplication Masters

Over 40 duplication masters, ready for individual use, to support many of the strategies explained in the book *Motivation & Learning*. Site licenses are available for considerable savings.

Workshops and Consulting

Workshops, consulting, and train-the-trainer sessions by the authors and their colleagues can be scheduled at your site. Each workshop will be custom-tailored to meet your specific needs and conducted in a manner consistent with best practices and research.

To order additional copies of this book, schedule presentations or workshops, or request information about any of the above resources, please call, fax, write, or e-mail Peak Learning Systems.

Telephone	303-679-9780
Fax	303-679-9781
Write	6784 S. Olympus Dr., Evergreen, CO 80439-5312
E-mail	Peaklearn@aol.com
Website	http://www.peaklearn.com